IMAGES
of America

LUKE AIR FORCE BASE

ON THE COVER: In 1954 and 1955, Luke Air Force Base added two large maintenance hangars south of the west ramp. Hangar 913, completed in 1954, is to the east, and Hangar 914, completed in 1955, is to the west. Taken on May 27, 1955, this photograph looks to the southeast and shows Hangar 913. Initially, maintenance personnel used this hangar for heavy maintenance on the F-84F Thunderstreak. (Courtesy of the US Air Force.)

IMAGES
of America

LUKE AIR FORCE BASE

Rick Griset

ARCADIA
PUBLISHING

Published by Arcadia Publishing
Charleston, South Carolina

Printed in the United States of America

Library of Congress Control Number: 2019949065

For all general information, please contact Arcadia Publishing:
Telephone 843-853-2070
Fax 843-853-0044
E-mail sales@arcadiapublishing.com
For customer service and orders:
Toll-Free 1-888-313-2665

Visit us on the Internet at www.arcadiapublishing.com

*To my lovely bride, Miss Cheryl, and to the men and women
who have served their country at Luke Field/Air Force Base.*

CONTENTS

ACKNOWLEDGMENTS

Since the opening of the Litchfield Park Army Air Field in 1941, an unknown number of people have helped preserve the history of Luke Air Force Base. Between 1951 and 2010, three full-time historians collected and wrote most of the base's histories: Jean Provence, Robert Sullivan, and Gustave Vinas. They created the Luke Air Force Base archive I used for this work. I want to thank the historical societies in the cities that surround Luke Air Force Base, especially its closest one, the Litchfield Park Historical Society, for their encouragement.

I also wish to thank my editors at Arcadia Publishing, Lindsey Givens, Stacia Bannerman, and Caitrin Cunningham.

Special thanks to Gary Boyd, the command historian for Air Education and Training Command, for his encouragement and guidance. Finally, a thank-you to my lovely bride, Cheryl, for your love and encouragement in all we do.

In an effort to support the present and future men and women of Luke Air Force Base, the author's royalties from this book will go to Fighter Country Partnership and the Frank Luke Jr. Memorial Museum.

All photographs are courtesy of the US Air Force and are official US Air Force photographs. If the photographer is known, credit is given.

INTRODUCTION

The Army built what became Luke Air Force Base in reaction to Pres. Franklin D. Roosevelt's call, during the 1940 Battle of Britain, for an increase to 12,000 new military pilots a year. The Del Webb Corporation built the base in 11 months. On June 6, 1941, the Army renamed Litchfield Park Army Air Field after World War I hero Lt. Frank Luke Jr. Over the course of 18 days in September 1918, Lieutenant Luke flew on 8 days. During that time, he shot down 14 balloons and 4 enemy aircraft, making him a triple ace. At the time of his death, he had more aerial kills than any other American flier, referred to in those days as the Ace of Aces. Luke's exploits earned him the first Medal of Honor given to an Army flier. By the end of the war, only Capt. Eddie Rickenbacker had more kills.

The base's flight training initially started at Sky Harbor Municipal Airport in Phoenix. On July 15, 1941, the entire school transferred from Sky Harbor to Luke Field for full-time operations. Prior to and during World War II, flight training occurred in three almost equal 10-week phases. First, a student went through primary flight training, taught by a civilian contract school. That training consisted of 65 flying hours (later reduced to 60 hours) and 175 landings in light aircraft like the Boeing/Stearman PT-13 and PT-17 Kaydet biplanes. Next came basic flight training.

Basic required more advanced skills to graduate. For one, it used a more advanced aircraft, the Vultee BT-13 Valiant. Divided into two parts, basic flight training totaled 70–75 flight hours. The first part was transition, where the student learned about his new aircraft. Next came the diversified phase, which required smooth control of the aircraft and precision flying. Here, the student learned how to fly acrobatics and accurate maneuvers. Training topics included formation flying, instrument flying, night flying, and cross-country flights. To help the students with those tasks, they started using the Link trainer. Near the end of the war, the Valiant was replaced with the AT-6 Texan.

After graduating from basic, students went on to advanced flight training. The Army Air Forces divided advanced training into two types of schools, single-engine and multi-engine. Single-engine graduates tended to go to fighters, and multi-engine graduates tended to go to bombers or transports. Luke Field was a single-engine advanced flight training school teaching cadets how to fly fighter-type aircraft. Early in 1942, the Chinese air force sent cadets to Luke Field to learn to fly fighters. The AT-6 Texan was the principal aircraft, with over 500 at the base during the war. Upon graduation, the cadets got their commissions and wings.

They then went to more training in a specific fighter aircraft. In 1942, Curtis P-40 Warhawk aircraft allowed the base to provide that specific follow-on training. Much later, Lockheed P-38 Lightning and North American P-51 Mustang aircraft came to Luke Field. In 1946, the Army closed Luke Field. During the postwar years, under Col. Barry M. Goldwater, the Arizona National Guard started using part of Luke Field.

In 1951, in reaction to the Korean War, the Air Force federalized Luke Air Force Base, Arizona Air National Guard's 197th Fighter Squadron, and the 127th Fighter Wing of the Michigan Air National Guard, bringing it to the base. Then, the Air Force redesignated the wing as the 127th Pilot

Training Wing. Thus began the jet age at Luke Air Force Base, with the Lockheed F-80 Shooting Star, its training version the Lockheed T-33 Shooting Star, and the Republic F-84 Thunderjet.

After 18 months, the 127th Pilot Training Wing defederalized, and the 3600th Combat Crew Training Wing took over control of Luke Air Force Base. In 1954, the wing established the aerial demonstration team, which became the world-famous Thunderbirds. One of the base's pilots won the cross-country Bendix Trophy race that year. It also started the training of German pilots to fly the F-84F Thunderstreak through the Military Assistance Program in 1957. The Germans would remain at the base for the next 26 years. That year also brought the North American F-100 Super Sabre to the base.

On July 1, 1958, Luke Air Force Base transferred from Air Training Command to Tactical Air Command. As part of the transfer, the 4510th Combat Crew Training Wing replaced the 3600th Combat Crew Training Wing. Starting in 1961, the North American F-86 Sabre came to the base, but it left within two years. In 1964, as part of the German air force's training, the F-84 left and the Lockheed F-104 Starfighter arrived. Also in 1964, the Northrop F-5A/B Freedom Fighter arrived, assigned to the 4510th Combat Crew Training Wing but stationed at Williams Air Force Base, Arizona.

In 1969, the Air Force did away with four-digit units and brought back combat designations, naming wings after World War II groups. On October 15, 1969, the 58th Tactical Fighter Training Wing took over Luke Air Force Base. That year, the Ling-Temco-Vought A-7 Corsair II arrived, but it left the base within two years. When the A-7s left, so did the F-100s. Taking their place on the parking ramp was the McDonnell Douglas F-4C Phantom II. On November 14, 1974, the first McDonnell Douglas F-15A/B/C/D arrived.

On April 1, 1977, due to a spate of command and control issues, Tactical Air Command stood up Tactical Training Luke to oversee the redesignated 58th Tactical Training Wing. On August 29, 1979, a sister wing, the 405th Tactical Training Wing, activated to share the load, taking on the F-15s, F-5s, and helicopters. On December 1, 1980, the 832nd Air Division replaced Tactical Training Luke. In 1982, the F-4Cs left, replaced by the Lockheed F-16 Fighting Falcon. In 1983, the F-104s left. In 1988, the McDonnell Douglas F-15E Strike Eagles arrived. In 1989, the F-5s departed.

On October 1, 1991, Luke Air Force Base reorganized under the one-base, one-boss concept. Both the 832nd Air Division and 405th Tactical Training Wing inactivated, and the redesignated 58th Fighter Wing took over again. Later that year, the last of the F-15A/B/C/D-model aircraft departed.

On April 4, 1994, the 56th Fighter Wing moved to Luke Air Force Base from MacDill Air Force Base, Florida. The redesignated 58th Special Operations Wing moved to Kirkland Air Force Base, New Mexico. In 1995, the last of the F-15E Strike Eagles left, turning the 56th Fighter Wing and Luke Air Force Base into the premier F-16 flying training wing and base. In 2014, the Lockheed Martin F-35A Lightning II began replacing the F-16s.

Since its very beginning, Luke Field/Air Force Base has trained airmen to be fighter pilots. It continues that training today. Luke Air Force Base is already the premier F-35A training base, with more F-35A aircraft assigned than any other wing or base. Over the decades, the base has tried to be a good community partner. In return, the surrounding 11 communities work with Luke Air Force Base for solutions to issues that satisfy both parties.

One

LUKE FIELD

1940–1946

Second Lt. Frank Luke Jr. stands in front of his 13th kill on September 18, 1918. It was his fifth kill that day. In 18 days in September 1918, Luke shot down 4 aircraft and 14 balloons, earning the nickname "the Arizona Balloon Buster." Luke was the first airman to earn the Congressional Medal of Honor. On June 6, 1941, the Army renamed Litchfield Park Army Air Field after Luke.

Taken on September 16, 1941, this photograph looking east shows Luke Field under construction with Camelback Mountain in the background. At center, the chapel is under construction. Gene Autry did his radio show from the chapel during the war. It is still in service today. In the foreground, beyond the telephone pole, the Del Webb Corporation soon built a theater and a swimming pool.

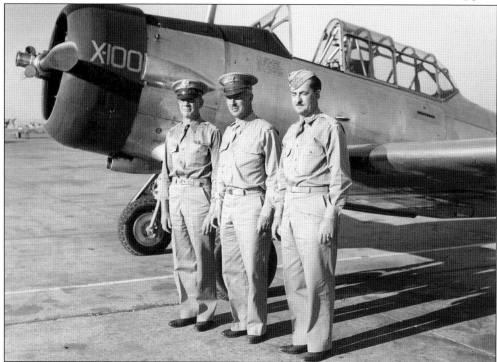

From left to right, Col. Ennis C. Whitehead, Lt. Col. William A.R. Robertson, and Lt. Col. Othel R. Derring stand in front of aircraft X-100. Whitehead was the father of Luke Field. He arrived on February 15, 1941, to command the Air Corps Advanced Flying School in Phoenix. He oversaw the construction of Luke Field, established the flying school, and moved the school to Luke Field.

After they moved from Sky Harbor airport in June 1941, airmen started flying the AT-6 Texan aircraft in the heat of the summer. With no hangars built yet, airmen maintained the aircraft on the flight line. They used grass huts for shade on and near the parking ramp. This photograph was taken from the control tower looking to the southwest.

Before buildings were completed, tents were used for several functions. This photograph, taken from the aircraft parking ramp, tells transient aircrews where to find Base Operations. Typically, transient aircraft park in front of Base Operations. With the fire hydrant in the foreground and the control tower in the background, this tent was a little south of where the Base Operations building was later constructed but close to where the two aircraft hangars were built.

Luke Field Exchange No. 1 was small and probably far away from the main exchange buildings. It was one of two small exchanges on base. The small sign next to the door reads "Hours 0900–1700 Daily Except Sundays & Holidays." Chances are it provided candy, coffee, cold soda pop, and tobacco products to flight line personnel like cadets, instructor pilots, and maintenance personnel.

During World War II, the Army held many military ceremonies to help build morale, often with troops marching in review. This review at Luke Field was similar to the September 29, 1941, ceremony held to formally dedicate Litchfield Park Field in honor of Frank Luke Jr. on the 23rd anniversary of his death. Otillia Luke, the aviator's mother, attended and spoke about her son's life.

On January 9, 1942, Cadet Richard "Dick" I. Bong completed North American AT-6 Texan advanced training at Luke Field as a member of Class 42-A. Upon graduation, Bong earned his wings and his commission as a second lieutenant. He stayed at Luke Field as a gunnery instructor. Later, he flew in the Pacific theater, becoming America's all-time ace with 40 kills and earning the Medal of Honor.

In January 1942, Second Lt. Richard "Dick" Bong flew the plane that took this iconic photograph over the Grand Canyon. Second Lieutenant D.R. Bridges flew the closest plane. Second Lt. James P. Johnson flew the middle plane. Second Lt. Jay MacBeall flew the plane farthest away. At that time, all four were instructors at Luke Field. Almost every class after that date included this photograph in its class book.

Part of Luke Field's construction plan was to create space for a sub-depot. On October 20, 1941, the first hangar built on Luke Field was under construction. It later housed the sub-depot's aircraft maintenance function. A sub-depot handled all local maintenance beyond the flight line along with supply. Today, the component maintenance squadron, equipment maintenance squadron, and logistics readiness squadron perform many of those same functions.

During World War II, the front gate was on the west side of Litchfield Road, where the Maj. Troy Gilbert Bridge is now. In this photograph, the gate guards salute the car entering the base. Behind the flagpole is the headquarters building, then Temporary Building T-11, built in 1942. It was later renamed Building S-11 and housed the headquarters until 2005. It is still in use today.

OVER 100,000 FLYING HOURS.

Flying 100,000 hours was and still is a substantial achievement. These original squadron commanders, assigned since June 6, 1941, completed 100,000 hours with their students in the AT-6 Texan at Luke Field on February 23, 1942. Amazingly, they flew those hours in under nine months. From left to right are Lt. Robert M. Wray, Capt. Joe H. Ashy, Capt. John C. Foster, Lt. N.R. Moon, base commander Col. Ennis Whitehead, Capt. W.L. Hall, Lt. B.B Zeran, and Capt. E.C. Kenyon.

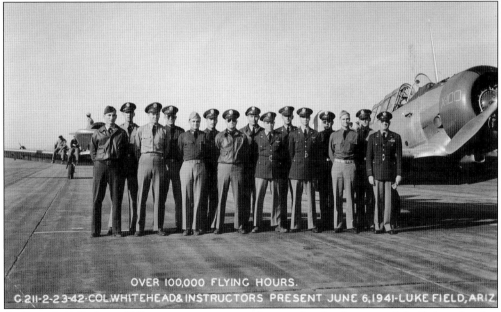

OVER 100,000 FLYING HOURS.
C.211-2-23-42-COL.WHITEHEAD&INSTRUCTORS PRESENT JUNE 6,1941-LUKE FIELD,ARIZ

On June 6, 1941, these 15 flying instructors were the initial cadre that moved the flying school to Luke Field from Sky Harbor airport. This photograph was taken on February 23, 1942. From left to right are Lts. Quentin Corley, Dave Cordy, Marty Mulligan, Bill Grund, Bob Burnett, Fergus Faye, Fred Elliott, Bob Fensler, Cliff Nesselrede, Jake Dyeneck, Bill Hite, Snuffy Smith, George Bosch, and Hugh Knoell, and base commander Col. Ennis Whitehead.

Prior to World War II, aviation caught the imagination of America. Originally, people saw pilots as daredevils and adventurers. In the interwar years, flying became the dream of many boys and girls. With President Roosevelt's call for thousands more military pilots, many young men got their chance to learn how to fly. Here stands an unidentified Luke Field aviation cadet during World War II.

A corporal prepares to release a weather balloon from Luke Field's weather section's tower. The weatherman has his hand on the instrumented telescope he will use to track the balloon. In that way, he could determine the winds at various altitudes. Within the box on top of the tower were the weather instruments. Note the "Explosive Gas" sign warning about the gas used to fill the balloon.

This class of Chinese air force cadets was in flying training at Luke Field. For China, World War II started in 1937 with the Japanese invasion. In early 1942, the first Chinese air force class arrived to learn to fly the AT-6 Texan. On March 27, 1942, the first class of 42 Chinese students graduated. By the end of the war, 508 Chinese cadets graduated in the AT-6.

Seven North American AT-6 Texans fly in formation over the Sonoran Desert and farmlands. In World War II, flying in large formations was an important skill. The large "X" identifies them as coming for Luke Field. The numbers identify the aircraft from a distance. The pilots are watching the lead pilot or the one next to them, helping them keep their speed, distance, and location in the formation.

On December 17, 1941, President Roosevelt increased the required number of military pilots to 30,000 per year. As a result, classes at Luke Field grew much larger in 1942 and 1943. This photograph shows the 330th School Squadron at Luke Field in 1942. Pilots typically went through primary training at contractor facilities, where they flew little. Next was basic flying training,

where they flew about 70 hours. Then, they went to advanced flying training, which was either single-engine like at Luke Field or multi-engine like at Williams Field in Mesa, Arizona. On the tarmac of the north parking ramp looking north, one can see the control tower on the right. The Army Air Forces reorganized the units on Luke Field several times during World War II.

This photograph looks southeast from the south control tower on February 9, 1943. Two-story barracks are in the foreground. In the near background on the right is the family housing area. In the far background behind the family housing area is South Mountain. In the far background on the left are Camelback Mountain and Squaw Peak, which in 2003 was renamed Piestewa Peak.

Here is a café on Luke Field where cadets went on breaks to get food, coffee, and milkshakes. The mural on the far wall captures elements of cadet life and their goal. From left to right are gunnery practice, athletics, an American pilot, the compass for navigation, a Chinese pilot, learning Morse code, academics, and the Link trainer.

The soda fountain in the Main Exchange served sandwiches, sodas, and ice cream. The two banks of milkshake machines were used to make malts and shakes. The most expensive sandwich on the menu boards was a ham and cheese for 20¢. Most other sandwiches cost 15¢, as did malts, shakes, and floats. Donuts, coffee, and sodas were all 5¢.

The soft drink counter in the exchange also sold snacks and beer. Base leadership restricted the sales of beer to between 5:00 p.m. and 9:00 p.m. According to the sign in this photograph, a beer cost 10¢. No other prices are visible. Aviation cadets received $75 a month. With that they had to pay for clothes, non–chow hall food, hobbies, and incidentals.

The ladies of the quick lunch counter in the B Street Branch await the hungry cadets. The cadets were young men with money in their pockets. The quick lunch counter offered coffee, sandwiches, chili with beans, sodas, ice cream sundaes, and tobacco products. The entry was on the right, with the exit through the turnstile on the left.

After the cadets bought their food, they often walked over to the stand-up tables in the B Street Branch. At far right, the water fountain stands next to the cigarette machine. What better way for busy cadets to grab a quick lunch than the quick lunch counter and its stand-up tables?

Due to segregation, the Army Air Forces had to have two of everything. This picture shows African Americans in the Post Exchange's segregated sandwich shop. The sandwich shop was part of the Third Street Exchange. A close look at the menu shows tuna or corned beef sandwiches were 15¢ each. Cheese or ham salad sandwiches were 10¢. The sandwich shop also served salads, milk, coffee, and sodas.

World War II cooks of the segregated 975th baked cakes for the visiting Joe Lewis, the reigning world heavyweight boxing champion. The cake on the left reads "Luke Field Welcomes You Joe." The one on the right reads "Welcome to Luke Field Champ." Beating Germany's Max Schmeling in 1938 made Lewis a national hero to both blacks and whites. In 1942, Lewis enlisted in the segregated US Army.

Part of the exchange system was the commissary, which had several small departments. Pictured here is the produce department. Baskets sit near the register, with Rainbow Bread toward the wall and the tavern shop on the wall to the right. The commissary also had meat and dairy departments. While cadets could use the commissary, families typically made up most of its customers.

This busy clothing department was in the Luke Field Main Exchange. While airmen received issued clothing, the clothing department was one place to buy better-quality clothing. Shirts are on the right. Hats are straight back behind the counter. Jackets and coats are on the far left. Pants hang in the center of the store. On the left, airmen sit in the shoe area with shoe boxes on the left wall.

Before personal communication devices, writing home was the way to stay connected with family. To do so, one needed stationery. The stationery department in the Luke Field Main Exchange offered stationery, envelopes, postcards, and pilot logbooks. It shared the counter with the jewelry department. The exchange offered a variety of other services, including a tobacco counter, a hobby counter, and a drugs and notions counter.

While the cadets typically did not have cars, many of the officers did. Gasoline was a rationed item during the war, but the prices on the gas station pumps show the most expensive grade was 20¢ per gallon. Situated just inside and north of the north gate, the exchange gas station was in building T-342. Other exchange services included barbershops, alteration and pressing departments, and even free bowling.

Flying in formation was and still is an important skill. Students practiced formation flying as one of the skills needed to earn their wings. When a flying squadron traveled as a unit, the formation could be sizeable. Here, 17 aircraft fly over Luke Field in formation. This is an excellent example of both vertical and horizontal separation required in formation flying.

In 1942, Luke Field began flying the Curtiss P-40 Warhawk. At the beginning of the war, it was the Army's top fighter aircraft. Chinese air force students were the first to train in the P-40 at Luke Field, followed shortly by American students. Curtiss manufactured the P-40 into 1944. By the end of the war, Luke Field graduated at least 2,483 American and 331 Chinese pilots in the P-40.

During a retreat ceremony at Luke Field in 1943, the US Army Air Forces Women's Auxiliary Corps unit formation commander is caught in mid-salute. They stand in front of the headquarters building with the water tower in the background. Although the number of servicewomen assigned at Luke Field was small, their contribution to the war effort was significant in that the tasks they performed freed men for combat.

During World War II, women held all kinds of jobs at Luke Field. Sitting in the cockpit of an AT-6 Texan is a ground trainer specialist, Sgt. Helena Donahue of the US Army Air Forces Women's Auxiliary Corps, checking the communications equipment. By taking on this job, she freed men to fill instructor and combat roles.

This undated photograph shows the main 87th Sub-Depot supply warehouse, Warehouse No. 1 at Luke Field. Most of the people in this photograph are women. The 87th Sub-Depot only stored small parts in Warehouse No. 1; it kept larger parts in the other warehouses. The offices are on the second floor at the back of the warehouse.

In the foreground, the aeronautical repair shop of the 87th Sub-Depot took aircraft apart and put them back together when they came in for overhaul. After overhaul, all aircraft needed a test flight. At upper left, the pre-flight shop prepares aircraft for flight after rebuild. All of the aircraft in this photograph are AT-6 Texans except for one B-25 Mitchell bomber in the background.

Two female teams vertically build Pratt & Whitney R-1340 Wasp radial aircraft engines in the 87th Sub-Depot engine shop on Luke Field. The AT-6 Texan used these engines. Behind them stands a parts bin for small engine parts as they disassemble and rebuild the engines. Behind the parts bin are two assembled Allison V-1710 V-12 engines used on the P-40 Warhawk aircraft. Beyond them are more assembled radial engines.

Two mixed-gender sheet metal teams work to rebuild the center sections of two wings for AT-6 Texan aircraft in the aero repair section of the 87th Sub-Depot. World War II required the involvement of the entire population. Most men ended up in the military. Women filled what were previously men's jobs. Collectively, those women became known as "Rosie the Riveter."

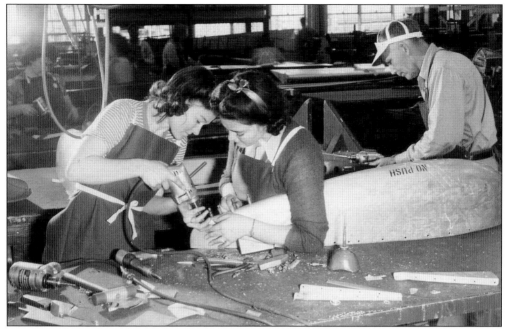

Two Rosie the Riveters put a wingtip back together in the 87th Sub-Depot sheet metal shop. They are drilling holes through the sheet metal and the frame below. The woman at center is holding a pin with her right hand. Those pins hold the pieces together until the riveters come back and rivet the pieces together. Several other women are working in the background.

The 87th Sub-Depot machine shop with its large lathes and other machines needed operators with skills, especially math skills. Machine shops like this one manufactured and repaired aircraft parts. Though the shops were traditionally male dominated, four of the twelve workers in this photograph are female. As was normal for the time, they lacked a lot of today's safety gear, which had not been invented yet.

While most of the aircraft was metal, some control surfaces were still fabric to save weight. By stretching fabric over a frame, applying dope, and letting it dry, a usable control surface was produced. Here, the 87th Sub-Depot doping room is busy. The windows are open and the fan is expelling air from the room. Anyone who has doped a model aircraft can understand why.

Pictured here is the 87th Sub-Depot parachute section. Little has changed in packing parachutes since World War II. The long tables are still used, as are the weighted bags that hold things in place. The people who pack parachutes are known as riggers; they rig the parachute to open when the wearer pulls the D-ring handle.

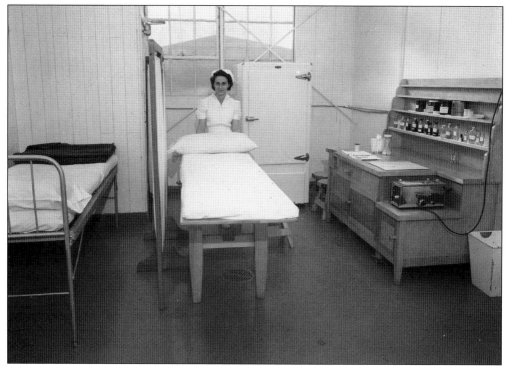

With all of the heavy machinery and the distance to the hospital at the southeast end of the base, the 87th Sub-Depot had its own first aid room. It could handle two patients at a time, and the nurse had a refrigerator to store medicines that had to be kept cold. Although the room was spartan, it was functional. The metal box on the counter was for sterilizing equipment.

Twenty-one members of the Luke Field Fire Department stand in front of Fire Station No. 1 with two of their firetrucks in this undated photograph. Given their apparent age, chances are most of the members are civilians. The two half-dome maintenance hangars in the background place the fire department across the street from the flight line, where the wing headquarters building is today.

Three AT-6 Texans fly in formation low over the Sonoran Desert. Each pilot keeps his eye on the leader. In this photograph, aircraft markings no longer match the tail numbers. From left to right, aircraft X-259 is tail number 41-32197, X-272 is tail number 41-3226, and X-267 is tail number 23906 or -8. The radio antenna runs from the post in front of the cockpit to the tail.

Late in the war, P-38 Lightning and P-51 Mustang training came to Luke Field. On March 13, 1945, P-38 fighter transition training began, and in July, P-51 fighter transition training started. On August 14, 1945, both programs ended at Luke Field. During their short stays, Luke Field graduated 280 American P-38 pilots and 61 P-51 pilots. The Chinese continued P-51 training until May 15, 1946.

Luke Field had eight auxiliary fields, four to the north and four to the south. Auxiliary Field 1, or Wittman Field, is still in use today. It is southwest of where the canal crosses Route 60 near West Patton Road. Auxiliary Field 2, or Beardsley Field, was just north of Route 60 and west of North 163rd Avenue. Auxiliary Field 3 was between Bell Road and Greenway Road just west of Litchfield Road, now the Surprise City Complex. Auxiliary Field 4, or Wickenburg Field, is northwest of the intersection of West Patton Road and North 259th Avenue. Auxiliary Field 5 is southwest of the intersection of South Palo Verde Road and West Yuma Road, now the Buckeye Municipal Airport. Auxiliary Field 6, or Goodyear Field, is northwest of the intersection of Yuma Road and South Verrado Way. Auxiliary Field 7, or Hassayampa Field, was west of the intersection of West Ward Road and West Salome Highway, now the Hickman Egg Ranch. Auxiliary Field 8 is about six miles due north of Ajo, Arizona, east of State Route 85, now Eric Marcus Municipal Airport.

Luke Field instructors and students flew one million hours in exactly 32 months. From left to right are Col. John K. Nissley, Luke Field's commanding officer; Lt. Col. Lester S. Harris, director of training; Maj. Hugh A. Griffith Jr., base operations officer; and Capt. William A. Payton, assistant operations officer. On February 7, 1944, the three others congratulate Colonel Nissley as he climbs out of his AT-6 Texan after flying the one millionth hour. One factor that allowed them to fly so many hours is that at times they had over 500 aircraft assigned to the base. To put their accomplishment into perspective, it took the F-16s over 30 years to fly a total of one million hours at Luke Air Force Base. Due to its large number of hours flown by the end of the war, Luke Field graduated at least 13,568 American and 508 Chinese pilots from advanced flying training in the AT-6.

For air-to-ground gunnery practice, the Army established the Gila Bend Gunnery Base as a sub-post of Luke Field. After his time at Ajo Army Air Field, Maj. Dewey Bartlo commanded the sub-post. He made major improvements including at Gila Bend's three auxiliary bases, numbered 4, 5, and 6, which were different than Luke Field's auxiliary fields. Now called Gila Bend Air Force Auxiliary Field, it is still in use today.

Over the Sonoran Desert's Gila Bend Range, a student makes a gunnery pass in his AT-6 Texan. His target is a large cloth banner with a circular bullseye. Pulling that target is another AT-6, probably from Ajo Army Air Field, Arizona. Aerial gunnery is an important skill for fighter pilots. During World War II, it was a primary offensive weapon and their only weapon in air-to-air combat.

Two

REACTIVATION AS LUKE AIR FORCE BASE

1951–1952

Standing in formation on July 22, 1950, at Selfridge Air Force Base, Michigan, is the 127th Fighter Wing (Michigan Air National Guard). Within seven months, that wing would be federalized, renamed, and moved to Arizona. On February 1, 1951, as the 127th Pilot Training Wing, it reopened Luke Air Force Base. There, it flew North American AT-6 Texans and F-51 Mustangs, Republic F-84 Thunderjets, and later, the Lockheed F-80 Shooting Star.

With the move of the 127th Pilot Training Wing from Selfridge Air Force Base to Luke Air Force Base and the start of daily flying, a lot of material needed to be brought in. In this photograph from February or March 1951, airmen unload crates from a truck with a forklift.

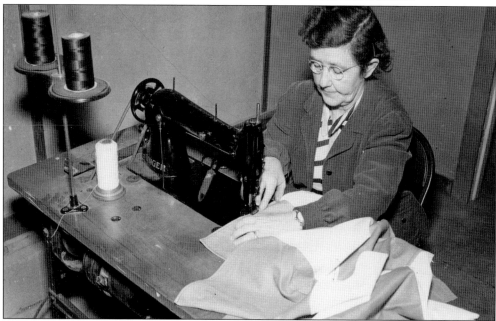

When the 127th Pilot Training Wing arrived at Luke Air Force Base, it needed airfield safety flags for vehicles and obstacles, especially around construction. Early in 1951, this seamstress is sewing together the standard orange-and-white three-foot-by-three-foot safety warning flags. Airmen would affix these warning flags to vehicles operating on the airfield as well as obstacles around the airfield.

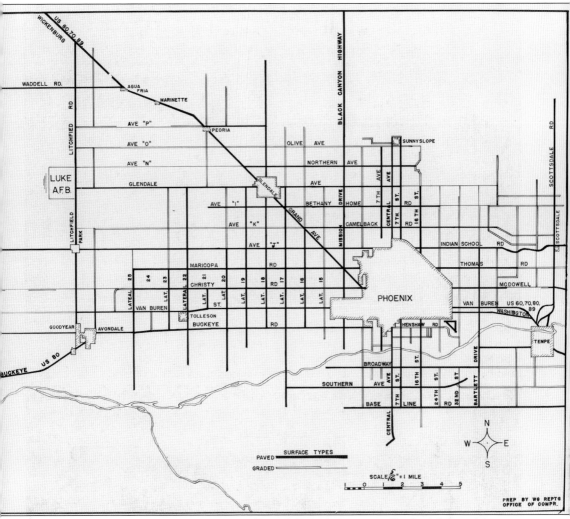

By March 31, 1951, Luke Air Force Base's Office of the Wing Comptroller had drawn this map. At that time, the only paved roads around the base were Litchfield Road, Glendale Avenue, Waddell Road, and Avenue J, later renamed Indian School Road. Most of the roads were graded dirt and look gray on this map. Most of the north-south roads still lacked names, indicating how rural the area was at that time. The quality of the Gila Bend Range and the open rural setting of the West Valley were two of the major reasons the Air Force reactivated the base. Litchfield Park was the only close town. Other than Phoenix, the largest town on the west side of the valley was Glendale, which was 10 miles away.

Two airmen in utility uniforms clean up around the 127th Headquarters Squadron Building, Temporary Building T-257 on Luke Air Force Base. The headquarters squadron carried out the administration functions for the people on the 127th Pilot Training Wing staff. After World War II, the Arizona National Guard owned Luke Field but only used a portion of the base's buildings. After reactivation, there was a lot of clean-up to do.

Besides cleaning up the base, many of the temporary World War II buildings needed repair and maintenance upon reactivation. In February or March 1951, the 127th Pilot Training Group Headquarters Building gets another layer of tarpaper and asphalt shingles to prevent the roof from leaking.

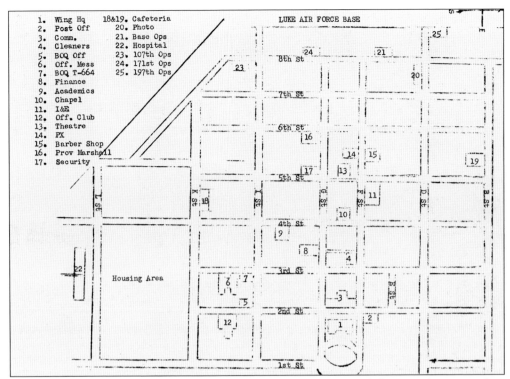

1.	Wing Hq	18&19.	Cafeteria
2.	Post Off	20.	Photo
3.	Comm.	21.	Base Ops
4.	Cleaners	22.	Hospital
5.	BOQ Off	23.	107th Ops
6.	Off. Mess	24.	171st Ops
7.	BOQ T-664	25.	197th Ops
8.	Finance		
9.	Academics		
10.	Chapel		
11.	I&E		
12.	Off. Club		
13.	Theatre		
14.	PX		
15.	Barber Shop		
16.	Prov Marshall		
17.	Security		

LUKE AIR FORCE BASE

Not surprisingly, many of the locations used during World War II had the same functions when the base reopened. Some examples were the wing headquarters building, the hospital, the theater, base operations, and the chapel. Of those, the last two still function in the same areas.

The Lockheed F-80 Shooting Star was the US Air Force's first operational jet fighter. On May 26, 1951, a squadron's worth of F-80 aircraft came to Luke Air Force Base. On November 13, 1951, those aircraft moved to Nellis Air Force Base in Nevada. They returned on February 25, 1952, as part of a split-phase training program. That split program ended on September 12, 1952.

Shortly after the 127th Pilot Training Wing arrived at Luke Air Force Base, this photograph was taken on March 18, 1951, looking to the southwest. The water tower is at lower left and the railroad tracks are at lower right. North American AT-6 Texan, North American F-51 Mustang, and Republic F-84 Thunderjet aircraft are on the north and south ramps on the far side of the buildings.

This 1951 photograph shows Luke Field looking east-southeast. The U-shaped building at lower left has a sign on its southern leg identifying it as base operations to transient aircraft. On the tarmac sit a North American AT-6 Texan and three Lockheed F-80 Shooting Stars. At right is a maintenance hangar, along with the north control tower and the empty World War II swimming pool.

42

After cleaning up Luke Air Force Base, airmen added new landscaping. Taken in 1951 from behind the main gate, this photograph shows the headquarters building, Temporary Building 11, in the background. Renamed Building S-11, it is still in use today. In the foreground is a memorial to decorated World War II graduates of Luke Field. The 24 panels of the memorial have been moved but are still on base.

This March 23, 1951, photograph shows Luke Air Force Base looking to the west. Extending from the concrete south ramp is the completed 8,800-foot-long, 120-foot-wide temporary asphalt jet runway running southeast to northwest parallel to the existing Runway 15/33. It was offset by 120 degrees from permanent Runway 03/21. The southwest end of Runway 03/21 is under construction so it could permanently handle jet aircraft.

Maintenance airmen swarm this Republic F-84F-15-RE Thunderstreak during an over-the-wing refueling. The Air Force stationed aircraft like this one at Luke Air Force Base between 1951 and 1964. Today, most crew chiefs would notice that this crew had no fireguard standing by with a bottle of fire retardant during refueling. Static electricity or a random spark can make refueling a dangerous operation.

In February or March 1951, a maintenance staff sergeant sits in the nose of an F-84 Thunderjet while working. He could be adjusting something, but chances are he is installing or removing a part. The ladder was used to get up to the nose, and the tags on the nose cover's latches are to remind the crew chief which latch is not fastened.

Col. David T. McKnight, the commanding officer of the 127th Pilot Training Group, greets 2nd Lt. Eugene Ruder, the first officer student to arrive at the reactivated Luke Air Force Base in 1951. After the Korean War started, the Air Force realized it needed more pilots and decided to reactivate Luke Field as an air force base.

On April 27, 1951, Second Lts. Daniel R. Lewellen, Raymon L. Koenig, and David S. Wittwer flew the first student training sorties at the reactivated Luke Air Force Base. The students flew their training sorties in a Republic F-84 Thunderjet. During the Korean War, the F-84 proved to be an excellent air-to-ground platform. The plane remained at the base from 1951 to 1964, making full use of the range.

To handle jet aircraft, Luke Air Force Base bought land to the southwest to extend Runway 03/21. On July 15, 1951, construction finished on the 8,800-foot permanent jet runway. Here, on March 20, 1952, the photographer is lined up with Runway 03. The asphalt taxiway is to the right.

This photograph was taken on July 28, 1951, shortly after the dike on the north side of Luke Air Force Base broke due to heavy rains in the area. In front of the people standing on the dike is a ditch, and closer to the camera is a dirt road, now Northern Avenue. At upper left is the flooded north aircraft parking ramp.

Pictured on August 3, 1951, six days after the north dike broke, Luke Air Force Base is still flooded, including the runway and buildings within an eighth of a mile of Litchfield Road. Family housing, transportation, and all of the headquarters functions are underwater. The new runway is at center. Flooding disrupted flying operations for two weeks.

In July and August 1951, the area experienced multiple heavy storms that flooded Luke Air Force Base at least three times. On the far side of the oval is the headquarters building. On the near side is the front gate along a flooded Litchfield Road. Due to the flooding, Glendale families took in airmen and their families for up to three weeks.

It seems odd to train for water survival in the desert, but in 1951, most Luke Air Force Base cadets would be flying somewhere else, like Korea. In those locations, water survival is a required skill. Shortly after the summer floods, this practical demonstration used an actual life raft. On August 10, 1951, a master sergeant demonstrates while a Mr. Cantwell explains how to use various pieces of equipment.

On July 19, 1951, a two-year-old girl got lost in the heat of the summer. Being good neighbors, the 127th Pilot Training Wing sent multiple busloads of airmen to assist in searching for the child. This photograph from July 20, 1951, captures the airmen getting organized to help with the search. Unfortunately, the search was unsuccessful, and organizers called it off the next day.

This photograph of base operations was taken on June 8, 1951. This is where transient aircrews go after arrival at the base and prior to departure. There they complete their postflight and preflight paperwork, including their flight plan. The large map on the wall is made up of a series of aviation flight maps cut and taped together to help the transient aircrews.

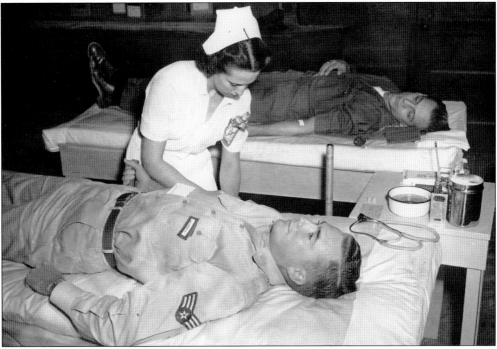

Donating blood is a well-established military activity that still goes on today. On September 26, 1951, a nurse draws blood from the sergeant in the foreground. The airman in the background is resting after giving his pint. After drawing blood, nurses still make donors rest for a few minutes so they do not pass out by standing too soon.

On September 7, 1951, maintenance takes apart an F-80 Shooting Star, tail number 51-527, for inspection. Like a car, aircraft require periodic maintenance and inspection. In 1951, airmen used a production-line concept to do that maintenance. Here, they remove the tail section so technicians can examine the engine and the structural integrity of the aircraft. In the background are one of the maintenance hangars and the north control tower.

In the production-line maintenance concept, each station accomplishes a different set of tasks. Sometimes maintenance rolls the aircraft between stations and the mechanics remain in place. Otherwise, the aircraft remains in place and the teams of mechanics rotate to each aircraft. On September 7, 1951, technicians at the electrical check station verify that all of the electrical wires and components are in working order.

Col. Henry J. Amen commanded the 127th Fighter Wing (Michigan Air National Guard) when it was federalized and redesignated. He brought the wing to Luke Air Force Base. On September 29, 1951, he held a base-wide open ranks inspection. Here, Colonel Amen inspects the officers of the wing headquarters. Every commander on base inspected each airman's uniform.

Later on a rainy September 29, 1951, Colonel Amen has the entire 127th Pilot Training Wing march in review. Here, he returns the salute of a parading squadron commander. As part of the salute sequence, all people in the ranks do an eyes-right except for the rightmost column. All flight leaders salute with the commander, and the squadron guidon lowers in salute.

51

On November 30, 1951, a photographer captured this simple mockup of the Republic F-84 Thunderjet fuel system with its three tanks. By using a mockup, the students learned what the gauges and dials looked like and where they were without tying up an aircraft. A fuel system that transferred improperly could cause weight and balance issues. At their extreme, those issues could cause the aircraft to depart controlled flight.

On December 7, 1951, Sgt. Robert S. Vanderford of the Synthetic Training Department communicates with a student pilot in a Link trainer during a simulated instrument flight in Korea. Students use Link trainers to work on their instrument flying. The black, triangular mechanism resting over the map is an automatic course plotter, which indicates the progress and position of the aircraft during the "flight." (Photograph by PFC Dale Tiderington.)

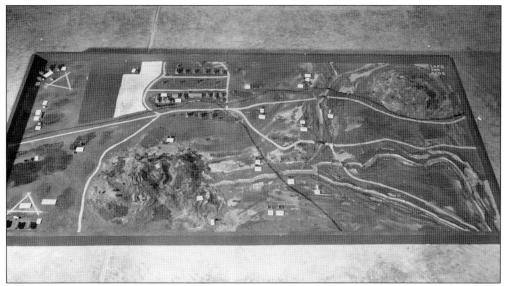

This October 4, 1951, photograph shows an airman's tactical operations mockup of a battlefield. Since most of the students would soon be in combat in Korea, it was important they understand how to conduct controlled air-to-ground operations. Labels identify the triangles on the left as a fighter (upper) and bomber (lower) airfields. Other tags identify the Army elements and their associated forward air controllers and tactical air control parties.

"When am I flying tomorrow?" is not a new question. This November 28, 1951, photograph shows the scheduling chalkboard of Section 3 of the 197th Training Squadron with six planned flights during the first three and a half hours of the day. After those flights land, depending upon how the students preform, the schedulers will fill in the rest of the day's flying training schedule.

Due to the urgencies of the war in Korea, lots of training occurred at the various bases as needed. On November 30, 1951, an instructor teaches a class of new clerk typists how to touch type on the typewriter. From the photograph, it is hard to tell whether the students are practicing or taking a timed test. Today, this type of class is referred to as keyboarding.

In fighter tactics, strafing is a required skill. On November 13, 1951, two airmen prepare a ground gunnery target for the Gila Bend Gunnery Range. They mop glue on the old target and roll the new target on top. Once dry, the targets will be placed on a frame on the gunnery range.

After each pilot finishes his strafing runs, airmen on the Gila Bend Gunnery Range score the targets. The closer the hole is to the center, or bull, the higher the score. In this November 13, 1951, photograph, an airman marks and counts the bullet holes in each scoring area. His marks will help him identify the new holes after the next pilot fires at the target.

During World War II, gun cameras became the standard verification device, especially for air-to-air engagements and claims of kills. On November 28, 1951, an instructor scores gun camera film as students watch. Given the time it takes to develop, dry, and spool the film, the feedback to students is not immediate. The instructor uses a compass to measure the distance between the tracer bullets and the intended target.

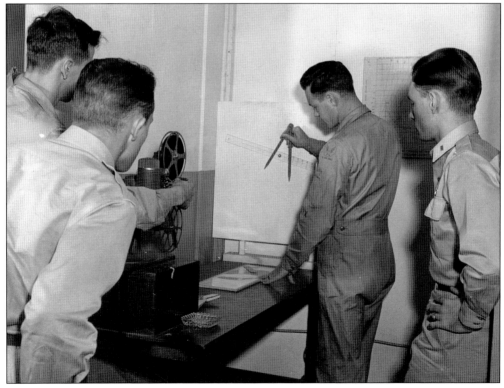

In 1951, baseball was still the national pastime. Many airmen grew up playing baseball and wanted to play after joining the Air Force. This photograph records the first organized recreation activity after the reactivation of Luke Air Force Base and was taken in February or March 1951. It shows a staff sergeant at bat wearing his utility coveralls with tennis shoes.

Taken in January 1952, this photograph shows the main gate looking due west. Very little new construction is evident. However, there is a new fire department building on the flight line between the hangar west of the empty pool and base operations, which is north of the hangar.

Three

3600TH COMBAT CREW TRAINING WING

1952–1958

Early in 1955, pilots from the 3600th Combat Crew Training Wing fly four General Motors F-84F Thunderstreaks in formation over the desert. Luke Air Force Base flew the F-84 from 1951 to 1964. During that time, the base graduated 6,930 F-84 pilots from training. Of the aircraft in the photograph, tail number 51-9319 crashed later in 1955, and tail number 51-9313 is currently on display at the Greater Peoria Airport, Illinois.

On August 21, 1952, in the heat of the summer at Luke Air Force Base, an instructor gives students a flight line briefing inside a cooler building. They would soon step out to fly a gunnery mission. Behind them is the flight scheduling board. It contains information like mission, pilot names, aircraft tail numbers, scheduled takeoff time, scheduled range, scheduled range times, and scheduled landing times.

On May 25, 1955, Luke Air Force Base maintenance personnel work to reconnect an F-84F Thunderstreak's tail pipe after an engine change. The exhaust gases from the J65 engine were hot enough to burn through aircraft structures. Therefore, Republic protected the aircraft by manufacturing tail pipes out of metals with high melting temperatures. Bicycles, like the one seen here, remained an important vehicle for maintenance personnel for the next 40 years.

Flying at the ground at 445 knots is one of the most dangerous things one can do with an airplane. Most people drive in two dimensions, but jet pilots fly fast in three dimensions. To help students think in three dimensions, the Luke Air Force Base Training Aids Section created this air-to-ground mission trainer. As the model flight lead pulls out of his dive, the wingman enters his.

The Luke Air Force Base Training Aids Section put this formation trainer together to help students understand what the various formations looked like. This photograph shows two four-ship formations. The slots in the base allow the instructors to change the models to match the various formations the students need to learn.

On July 26, 1952, the afternoon harmonization maintenance crew at Luke Air Force Base gets ready to do a periodic test on the accuracy of an F-84F Thunderjet's .50-caliber guns and sights. During the test, the man in the cockpit fires one gun at a time. From left to right are Airman Third Class David L. Drew, Staff Sgt. Fred T. Humiston, Airman First Class Quentin Brown, Airman Third Class Richard H. McKnight, and Airman Third Class Steve Hamas. (Photograph by A2C Fred Chapman.)

On May 26, 1952, after the first burst from the F-84F's .50-caliber nose gun on the harmonization range at Luke Air Force Base, Staff Sgt. Nathan Heard Jr. places his target marker. In the cockpit, the maintenance man adjusts the gun's sights, thus increasing its accuracy. The two-aircraft harmonization range was connected to and southwest of the south ramp and due south of the north ramp. (Photograph by A2C Fred Chapman.)

In December 1952, the Camouflage Range on the Gila Bend Range received an upgrade in simulated targets. Typically created out of plywood, nails, and paint, the targets simulate whatever the current threat is that pilots will face in combat. In this case, the target is a camouflaged Soviet tank. The Camouflage Range helps pilots identify enemy targets when those targets are made to be hard to find.

Taken in December 1952, this photograph shows two simulated targets on the Camouflage Range within the Gila Bend Range complex. In the foreground is a simulated anti-aircraft artillery gun. In the background are two simulated field guns. Made of plywood, poles, and paint and made to look like Soviet-issued guns, these camouflaged targets helped train pilots who would soon be in combat in Korea.

On May 25, 1953, Luke Air Force Base formed an aerial demonstration team soon called the Thunderbirds flying the straight-wing Republic F-84G Thunderjet. From left to right are (first row) Maj. Richard C. Catledge, team commander; (second row) Capts. Cuthbert A. Pattillo, Bob Kanaga, and Charles C. Pattillo. Alternate pilot Capt. Robert S. McCormick stands behind. Not shown are maintenance officer 1st Lt. Aubrey D. Brown and information officer Capt. Bill Brock.

In 1953, one of the first formations the Thunderbirds perfected was the diamond formation. Left and right wingmen followed the lead pilot. The slot pilot flew the back tip of the diamond. In Native American folklore of the Southwest, the thunderbird was a creature that ruled the skies. Typically a hawk or an eagle, it sent lighting and thunder from its eyes. During war, the thunderbird arranged victories.

In August 1953, Capt. Bob Kanaga left the Air Force. Capt. Robert S. McCormick became the slot pilot, and the team's original maintenance officer, 1st Lt. Aubrey D. Brown, added the duties of alternate pilot. From left to right in this August 1953 photograph are Brown, McCormick, Capt. Cuthbert A. Pattillo, team commander Maj. Richard C. Catledge, and Capt. Charles C. Pattillo. This team remained together until March 1954.

In 1954, the second Thunderbird team formed, still flying the straight-wing F-84G. The Pattillo brothers both left and were replaced by Capt. John R. Spaulding Jr. flying left wing and Lt. Wilber L. Creech flying right wing. Capt. Bill Brock, the information officer, also departed, and 1st Lt. Al Davis replaced him. They continued to wow crowds with their close precision flying just as the Thunderbirds do today.

On May 25, 1955, Lieutenant Procter briefs students on the F-84 cockpit layout and instruments. Cockpit layout is one of the first things students learn. Using photographs, the instructor can teach multiple students at a time. This frees up an aircraft for the flying schedule. The classroom also is much cooler and quieter than the flight line at that time of year, when temperatures often reach 100 degrees Fahrenheit.

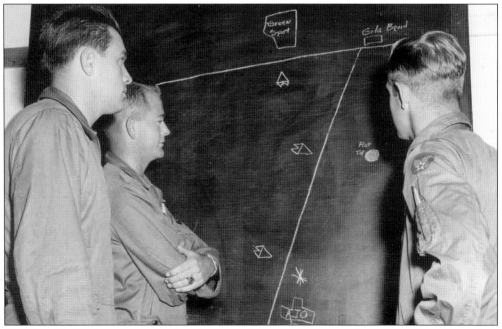

On May 25, 1955, an instructor briefs two students on navigation for a gunnery mission they are about to fly. On his simple map, the north-south line is Arizona State Route 85 between Gila Bend and Ajo. The triangles represent old auxiliary airfields and simulated airfields. Hat Mountain is most likely the flat-topped feature drawn on the board. Their target is the asterisk.

Throughout early aviation history, cross-country speed competitions were popular. On September 4, 1954, Capt. Edward W. Kenny of Luke Air Force Base won the Bendix Trophy air race in a Republic F-84F Thunderstreak. He set a course record of three hours and two minutes, averaging 616 miles per hour from Burbank, California, to Cleveland, Ohio. Previous winners included Maj. Jimmy Doolittle (1931) and Jacqueline Cochran (1938).

On July 7, 1954, the contractor finished the second 10,000-foot parallel hard-surface runway at Luke Air Force Base. With the high operation tempo, the base needed a second runway in case an incident tied up the primary runway or it was under repair. The newer jet aircraft were heavier and faster, requiring longer prepared surfaces for landing. This photograph was taken in 1957.

On May 21, 1955, Luke Air Force Base celebrated Armed Forces Day with an open house. Looking north, this photograph shows the northern half of the north ramp. At center right is the fire department's tower for drying hoses. The ambulance probably means that the fire department was also used as the first aid station. East of the World War II 87th Sub-Depot hangar is the parachute shop tower.

Five days after the open house, Luke Air Force Base hosted a Cub Scout pack. Here, the Scouts pose atop an F-84G similar to the aircraft the Thunderbirds just gave up. That spring, the Thunderbirds transitioned to the swept-wing F-84F Thunderstreaks. Throughout the history of the Air Force, many of its leaders were Boy Scouts first.

On May 27, 1955, the 3600th Combat Crew Training Wing's fighter gunnery team scores a tow target at Luke Air Force Base. From left to right are Capt. Samuel H. Chewning, Capt. Horace J. Mitchell, Col. Marvin E. Childs, and Capt. Richard E. Little (kneeling). It is still common for bases to have gunnery or bombing teams and hold competitions. Sometimes they are small affairs, and sometimes participants come from all over the Air Force.

After completing his training flight on May 25, 1955, a student checks back in at the squadron desk at Luke Air Force Base. His instructor pilot waits his turn to sign in. Afterwards, they will go to a briefing room and debrief the training mission. During debriefing, they will go over all aspects of the mission, and the instructor will critique the student's performance.

Maintenance conducts a quick turn on an F-84F, possibly during the Bendix Race. With the pilot in the seat and the engine running, maintenance personnel connect the refueling hose to the aircraft on the left. Crew chiefs check the tires. They also stand on a maintenance stand to either talk to the pilot or to reload the gun with ammunition. The fire trucks stand by, just in case.

On May 25, 1955, four weapons technicians, led by a technical sergeant, reload the .50-caliber gun magazine in the nose of an F-84F Thunderstreak at Luke Air Force Base. Until well after air-to-air missiles came into use, gunnery skill was critical in air-to-air engagements and strafing ground targets. The Gila Bend Range being so close was a major factor in the reopening of Luke Air Force Base.

The first 15-student class of German air force pilots began training in the F-84 at Luke Air Force Base on August 23, 1957. Seven were aces. From left to right are Capt. Friedrich Obleser, 20 kills; Lt. Col. Guenther Rall, 275 kills; Capt. Paul Schauder, 20 kills; Capt. Fritz Wegner, 8 kills; Maj. Erich Hartmann, 352 kills; Capt. Dieter Bernhard, 8 kills; and 1st Lt. Gerd Tetteroo, 9 kills.

On October 29, 1957, Col. Warren H. Higgens, commander of the 3600th Flying Training Wing, stands in front of the first F-100 Super Sabre at Luke Air Force Base shortly after its arrival. The F-100 was the first supersonic jet stationed at the base and would remain until 1971. In fact, 16 months earlier, the Thunderbirds moved to Nellis Air Force Base, Nevada, so the team could fly the F-100.

On October 21, 1957, prior to flight, two German students check out their helmets and parachutes from an airman second class working in life support. Life support's job is to fit the gear to the individual pilot or aircrew, maintain that gear, issue it prior to flight, and receive it after flight. Life support airmen understand the critical nature of their jobs. Pilots' lives depend upon them being thorough.

On May 25, 1955, two airmen second class inspect the vertical stabilizer of an F-84F. Previously, the vertical stabilizers were a problem on the F-84s. Chances are the fix included the periodic inspections pictured here. Part of the inspection is to ensure the cables controlling the vertical stabilizer are adjusted properly and not frayed. They likely added lubrication to any pivot surfaces, pullies, or bearings.

Four

4510TH COMBAT CREW TRAINING WING
1958–1969

Pictured on August 31, 1959, the main gate faces Litchfield Road. The buildings between the headquarters building, S-11, which is on the other side of the oval, and the chapel would be replaced in the later 1980s with the Air Park. The large building in the upper right is the gymnasium. The empty lot on the left is where the contractor is about to build a new dormitory.

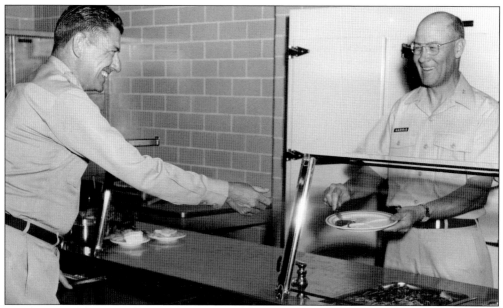

An old saying states that an army travels on its stomach. The same is true for the Air Force. On June 1, 1959, Luke Air Force Base opened a new airman dining hall. To commemorate the occasion, Col. Thomas W. Harris, commander of the 4510th Air Base Group, dishes the first serving to Col. Henry W. Terry III, deputy commander of the base.

Pictured on August 25, 1958, Northern Avenue runs along the top. East of Litchfield Road, contractors are moving dirt in preparation for a new housing area. Major changes were coming to Luke Air Force Base. While it was still a fairly isolated location, with all three aircraft parking ramps full of aircraft, the base needed places to house all of its people.

In 1959, two pilots of the 4510th Combat Crew Training Wing discuss a day's fighter training mission at the base operations facility at Luke Air Force Base. The 4510th Combat Crew Training Wing is part of Tactical Air Command. The increase in the base's elevation since 1941 is probably due to advancing technology and changing the measurement method, or the referenced point of origin.

Sen. Barry M. Goldwater, an Air Force Reserve officer, climbs into a F-100 for a check ride at Luke Air Force Base. Early in World War II, Goldwater served at Luke Field. In 1946, he helped establish the Arizona Air National Guard at Luke Air Force Base. Later, he became a major general in the Air Force Reserves. In 1964, he ran for president against Lyndon B. Johnson.

An airman loads 20-millimeter ammunition into the gun system of an F-100 aircraft at Luke Air Force Base in 1959. Due to gunnery's importance to fighter tactics, pilots at Luke Air Force Base shot thousands of rounds each month. This airman is loading a short belt of 10 rounds, probably during periodic maintenance, to ensure the loading system works properly.

Jet aircraft fires are primarily petroleum fires. They put off great heat and thick black smoke and carry other hazards like unexploded ordnance. On September 27, 1959, firefighters practice fighting an aircraft fire using a frame in the general shape of an aircraft. To practice their firefighting techniques, they douse the frame with petroleum and set it afire. This type of training continues today.

Many of the officers who underwent fighter pilot training at Luke Air Force Base went on to became leaders of the Air Force. In this 1959 photograph, 2nd Lt. Michael Dugan is the student in the foreground. On March 31, 1981, Colonel Dugan took command of the 832nd Air Division at Luke Air Force Base. In July 1990, General Dugan became the 13th chief of staff of the Air Force.

On July 5, 1960, the F-86 program along with its Lockheed T-33 Shooting Star lead-in phase moved to Luke Air Force Base from Williams Air Force Base, Arizona. By the end of the year, 30 F-86s were on station. They did not stay long. On September 27, 1962, the program moved to Nellis Air Force Base, Nevada. All told, 123 students from nine countries graduated from the course.

In the late 1950s, Luke Air Force Base replaced its World War II temporary family housing with a multi-housing unit design known as Capehart housing, pictured here. In September 1959, the base opened up the 724-unit Saguaro Manor housing area east of Litchfield Road and north of Glendale Avenue. In February 1971, the base opened up another 150 family housing units called Ocotillo Manor south of Glendale Avenue.

On October 27, 1959, Universal Construction Company turned over three new dormitories for airmen. The new dormitories allowed airmen to leave the nearly 20-year-old wooden temporary facilities built in 1941. This photograph, taken on January 21, 1960, shows the dormitory in use. Dormitories like this one remained in service for over 30 years.

On June 10, 1960, the Phoenix Air Defense Sector moved into a new building along Litchfield Road, Building 1150. Known as the "Blockhouse," its 16-inch reinforced concrete walls could withstand a near miss by a nuclear weapon. The Phoenix Air Defense Sector is Luke Air Force Base's largest tenant unit. On the sign, SAGE stands for Semi-Automatic Ground Environment. The Blockhouse now houses numerous base support functions.

Taken on July 11, 1960, this photograph shows the completed Saguaro Manor housing area. At the bottom is Luke Elementary School. Next to Litchfield Road is the newly completed Blockhouse. To the south of the hangars along the west ramp is the engine shop building. Only farmland and desert surround the base.

Looking east from the west ramp at Luke Air Force Base on January 12, 1960, students and instructor pilots preflight their T-33 aircraft. The T-33 is the trainer version of the United States' first jet fighter, the F-80. Although never a primary aircraft at the base, the T-33 was a safe lead-in jet for students prior to flying more dangerous jets like the F-100, parked in the background.

On April 29, 1960, three F-100s take off in formation at Luke Air Force Base. Formation takeoffs are another skill required of pilots. In combat situations, formation takeoffs allow pilots to get airborne quickly. At least one of these aircraft has a student pilot at the controls. Formation takeoffs are not easy and are briefed in detail prior to flight.

On May 26, 1960, airmen from Luke Air Force Base go through small arms training at a desert range. The airmen are firing a version of the M1 carbine as the instructors stand behind giving pointers on how to operate the weapon properly. A shooter's vision, breathing, trigger pull, and sighting of the weapon affect each shot.

On April 29, 1960, three airmen remove the nose landing gear strut from an F-100 at Luke Air Force Base. There are a number of reasons to remove a strut. Upon landing, the struts withstand a great deal of force. These mechanics may need to inspect where the strut is mounted to the aircraft or to repack the strut so it does not leak.

Members of the 4515th Combat Crew Training Squadron score an aerial gunnery target at Luke Air Force Base in 1961. The two pilots kneeling on the target are still wearing their G-suits. The Air Force highly encourages all kinds of competition. Chances are there are quarters bet upon this result.

On January 12, 1962, the wing scheduling officer, on the right, is hard at work trying to figure out how to get each pilot the training he needs. The technical sergeant is helping him. Students receive training in a certain sequence depending upon their experience and the course they are taking. It is the scheduling officers' job to maximize that training for operations.

Inside the 4510th Maintenance and Supply Group at Luke Air Force Base in 1961 is the nerve center of the maintenance complex: the maintenance control center. Each board controls a portion of the maintenance organization. The senior controller sits on the raised platform and is responsible for the execution of all scheduled maintenance actions. Controllers move pieces on the large board on the wall to show where the aircraft are.

On May 9, 1961, a Kaman H-43B Huskie takes off from Luke Air Force Base. At that time, the base owned various aircraft that supported the pilot training effort. For the most part, the base used helicopters to ferry range officers to and from the manned ranges. The H-43Bs flew at Luke Air Force Base from April 1960 to September 1961. They transferred out that fall.

On May 29, 1961, Brig. Gen. James W. Chapman Jr., commander of the 4510th Combat Crew Training Wing at Luke Air Force Base, congratulates Capt. Walter G. McMeen on his achievement. Four days earlier, Captain McMeen, a Luke Air Force Base helicopter pilot, flew an Air Force H-43B Huskie helicopter at Bloomfield, Connecticut, to an altitude of 25,814 feet, setting a new world record. A Russian held the previous record at 24,491 feet.

In 1961, maintenance facilities continue to extend along the west ramp at Luke Air Force Base. Parked to the east of the periodic maintenance hangars are F-84s, F-100s, and T-33s. From left to right are Hangars 913, 914, and two F-86 hangars under construction. Beyond Hangar 914 is the engine shop and engine test cell. Paul Litchfield's home, La Loma, is in the distance, as are South and Estrella Mountains.

On May 9, 1961, the engine test cell at Luke Air Force Base has an engine ready for a maximum run. On the right, the test engine is under the hoisting frame. To the engine's left is the control cabin. The earthen berm behind protects the nearby housing area and deflects the running engine's noise. The containers on the far left are cases used to transfer and store engines.

On May 9, 1961, a staff sergeant in the Luke Air Force Base Communications Center types a message in the Teletypewriter Exchange Service, or TWX, commonly referred to as a "twix." Similar to the telephone system, airmen use TWX to send official text messages between bases. Since communications are critical to military success, the Teletypewriter Exchange Service is an important system to the Air Force.

In 1964, when teaching larger classes as the war in Southeast Asia heated up, instructors at Luke Air Force Base needed large mockups that all of the students could see. Here, a student in the 4516th Combat Crew Training Squadron practices how to select the correct control switch on the armament control panel for one of the various munitions the F-100 carried.

In 1964, a technical sergeant working in the simulator at Luke Air Force talks a student through how to fly a jet fighter. Over the years, simulators improved. As of this date, large computers help the technicians run the cockpit instruments so the instruments react together as they would in flight. Technicians use that capability to simulate in-flight emergencies so the pilots can practice their emergency procedures.

On April 30, 1964, Maj. Gen. John C. Meyer, 12th Air Force commander and World War II quadruple ace, presides over the formal acceptance ceremony for the first F-5A Freedom Fighter in the Air Force inventory. The US F-5 Foreign Military Sales training program used F-5A/B aircraft and, later, F-5E/F Tiger II aircraft. On June 21, 1989, the program ended after producing 1,499 formal course graduates.

During the late 1950s and early 1960s, the F-84s from Luke Air Force Base routinely made very low passes on the Luke Air Force Range. This F-84 is pulling off the target on a live fire mission. Live fire missions are often the students' "final exam." The Soviet threat was real to the Western European students. To survive, many pilots wanted to fly fast and very high or very low.

On January 27, 1964, three instructor pilots in the 4514th Combat Crew Training Squadron work on the student training schedule at Luke Air Force Base. Operations scheduling is always a house of cards. If a scheduled pilot is unable to fly, often the entire schedule falls apart and must be rebuilt. With student training, the flying schedule is even more dynamic—tomorrow's missions depend upon the student's performance today.

On February 19, 1964, the airmen of a combat crew training squadron operations section track how the flights are going. The airman first class on the left talks to the pilots on the radio, and the airman first class on the right prepares to write down the takeoff time while the squadron's Top 3 (squadron commander, director of operations, and assistant to director of operations) watches.

On January 27, 1964, two airmen at Luke Air Force Base look to identify a needed part for a mechanic. The board displays various commonly used small parts and identifies their storage locations, which keeps the mechanics from rummaging through numerous bins to find the part. These boards are common in many maintenance areas. The racks of empty coke bottles indicate that the airmen also run the organization's unofficial snack bar.

Two F-104 aircraft take off to the northeast from Luke Air Force Base. The F-104s came to the base as a foreign military sales case. Germany bought them and replaced their F-84 training at Luke Air Force Base with F-104 flying training. While at the base, the German aircraft flew with US Air Force markings. The Mach 2 F-104 was known as "the missile with a man in it."

On August 20, 1969, German pilots hold a sign celebrating the 100,000th flying hour in the Lockheed F-104 Starfighter at Luke Air Force Base. The F-104s accomplished the feat in 64 months, averaging approximately 1,500 flight hours a month.

In 1968, with grease pencils, a technical sergeant and a staff sergeant update the control board in the command post on Luke Air Force Base. Both sergeants are talking to the flying squadrons, getting the latest information about the flying day. In the 1960s, Air Force leadership believed centralized control was the most efficient way to conduct business.

On December 12, 1967, an airman first class checks a rack of 2.75-inch rockets in the bomb dump at Luke Air Force Base. Unguided rockets like these were common weapons in the war in Southeast Asia. Therefore, fighter pilots training at Luke Air Force Base needed experience in their use. Pilots fired the rockets from pods attached to pylons under the aircraft.

On a hazy day looking north in late 1968, an F-100 flies low over Luke Air Force Base. All three aircraft parking ramps are full of F-100 aircraft, with the German F-104s on the far end of the north ramp. The north and south ramps are lined with maintenance hangars. In the foreground are the harmonization pads, while north of the base is only farmland.

On September 1, 1969, the first production Ling-Temco-Vought A-7D Corsair arrived at Luke Air Force Base. The crew chief talks to the pilot, Maj. Charles W. McClarren, after parking the aircraft. McClarren was commander of Detachment 1, 4525th Fighter Weapons Wing. A month later, the 58th Tactical Fighter Training Wing replaced the 4510th Combat Crew Training Wing as the host unit for Luke Air Force Base.

Using Luke Air Force Base as the main base, Operation Haylift loaded, flew, and air-dropped hay bales out of C-119 cargo aircraft like this one to starving Navajo cattle below. Between December 1967 and March 1968, the Navajo Nation in northern Arizona had so much snow that its cattle herds were threatened. To assist the Navajo, the Air Force organized four Operation Haylift efforts.

Five

58TH TACTICAL FIGHTER TRAINING WING
1969–1977

Typical fighter wings fly one type of fighter. After 1974, the 58th Tactical Fighter Training Wing flew four different fighters, leading to control issues. From top to bottom are an F-15A, tail number 76-078; an F-4C, tail number 63-420; an F-104, tail number 63-13269; and an F-5A, tail number 70-1396. On August 29, 1979, the 405th Tactical Training Wing activated at Luke Air Force Base to take over F-15 and F-5 training.

In 1970, the engine shop, built in 1959, was a block south of Hangar 913 at Luke Air Force Base. Aircraft fly based upon a combination of lift, drag, and thrust. Engines provide the thrust. Engine shop mechanics repair engines and remove and replace components. For badly worn or damaged engines, the shop packages and ships them to the depot for a complete teardown and rebuild.

Looking northeast in 1970, Luke Air Force Base has four jet engine sound suppressors. To fully test rebuilt engines, the test cell runs them through their various settings, including afterburner. At higher thrust settings, jet engines are loud. Prior to a test run, mechanics place the engine's tail in a suppressor, which uses a series of baffles to reduce the amount of noise.

With the northwest at top, this early 1970s overhead photograph of Luke Air Force Base shows more changes. South of Glendale Avenue is Ocotillo Manor. In the old World War II housing area is the officer's club, the new chapel, and the airmen's recreation center. The area south of the west ramp is filling in. Additionally, the northeast corner of Dysart and Glendale Avenues has commercial salt ponds.

On December 16, 1969, Col. John J. Burns, commander of the 58th Tactical Fighter Training Wing, sits in his A-7D at Luke Air Force Base. Shortly after this photograph, Congress announced the plane's departure. Nineteen months later, the A-7s departed for Davis-Monthan Air Force Base, Arizona. On July 20, 1971, the last A-7 class graduated, and the aircraft transferred. In less than 22 months, the 310th Fighter Squadron graduated a total of 143 A-7 students.

From the World War II days, when airmen were segregated by race, to today, the path of inclusiveness has had many steps. From the 1960s through the 1990s, more and more women joined the Air Force, filling traditionally male roles. In the fall of 1970, a chief master sergeant at Luke Air Force Base talks to an all-female class at leadership school. Mixed classes would occur later.

In the fall of 1970, instructor Lieutenant Colonel Delauter describes the left panel of the F-100 cockpit to a student at Luke Air Force Base. Enlarged photographs of the cockpit panels allow more students to learn the cockpit layout at the same time. Memory work has always been a critical part of being a pilot. Students still "chair fly" their missions the night before their check flights.

On November 2, 1971, an airman of the 58th Security Police Squadron stands guard on a F-4C at dusk at Luke Air Force Base. Thousands of people work on the base. Additionally, there are well over 100 aircraft on the aircraft parking ramps worth millions of dollars each. Guarding their safety means physical security on Luke Air Force Base is always a serious concern.

On April 15, 1970, Col. John V. Back, deputy commander for operations at Luke Air Force Base, examines a strike target through an instrument at Luke Air Force Range. On the manned ranges, the instrument allows the range officers to score the targets quickly from the range control tower while the aircraft are in the air and give that information back to the pilots prior to their next pass.

On August 17, 1971, the maintenance officer and a technical sergeant go over the aircraft forms for this F-4C, tail number 63-7675. A specialist recently completed a repair and signed the forms. A journeyman then reviewed the repair and signed that it was done correctly. Prior to flight, a supervisor reviews the forms for all repairs and checks corrective actions to ensure the aircraft is safe to fly.

On November 2, 1971, a master sergeant supervises the tow of an F-4C, tail number 63-7471. Towing aircraft is a daily occurrence at Luke Air Force Base. To prevent aircraft damage, tow teams require at least four people: the tow supervisor, the tug driver, and a wing walker for each wingtip. Backing the aircraft requires a tail walker. Any of them can stop the tow at any time.

Looking southeast at Luke Air Force Base's front gate in the late 1960s or early 1970s shows five static aircraft. Between the gate and the headquarters building is an F-84 aircraft painted like a Thunderbird. Clockwise on the street corners, the aircraft are an F-100, an F-86, another F-86, and an F-104. Today, all of the static aircraft on base are in the Air Park.

In 1972, airmen enjoy Soul Food Day at the noncommissioned officer's club at Luke Air Force Base as part of Black History Month, now African American History Month. For special events, the clubs offer different cuisines for a meal or a day. They serve corned beef and cabbage on St. Patrick's Day; for Cinco de Mayo, they serve Mexican food. Many clubs also frequently hold Mongolian barbecue nights.

On November 2, 1971, a crew chief in a "bunny suit" inspects the afterburner section of a J-79 engine on an F-4C at Luke Air Force Base. After every flight, crew chiefs carefully examine jet engines from both ends for anomalies like cracks, melted spots, or missing pieces. Often, the crew chief climbs into the afterburner section while it is still ticking as the metal cools after flight.

On November 2, 1971, a weapons crew uploads a rocket pod on an F-4C at Luke Air Force Base. A staff sergeant leads his dedicated crew and prepares to activate the hooks that lock the pod's lug nuts into place. After the May 16, 1965, disaster at Bien Hoa Air Base, South Vietnam, load crews could only use dedicated members who passed certification as a crew.

Luke Air Force Base sits at the west end of the large Salt River Valley, created by the Gila, Salt, Verde, and Agua Fria Rivers. That fact, combined with the occasional torrential rains, leads to flooding at various points all over the valley. Starting on June 22, 1972, heavy rains flooded parts of the north Phoenix valley. Since the city of Phoenix sits north of the Salt River, the water also flooded the city. Above, on July 5, 1972, helicopters from the base fly rescue missions to help their neighbors. Below, the next day, airmen drive large trucks through the flood waters to rescue people in Paradise Valley, northeast of downtown Phoenix.

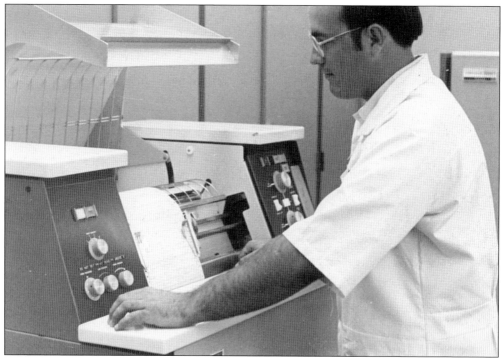

On July 19, 1972, an airman computer operator reads a printout from the Univac 1050 supply accounting computer at Luke Air Force Base. By the early 1970s, the Air Force had computerized its base-level supply systems. Each base had a Univac 1050 to handle its supply function. Computerization made accounting within the base supply system much easier and faster.

On February 28, 1972, a sergeant in the 58th Transportation Squadron tire shop at Luke Air Force Base fills a new tire just placed on the rim with air. The old tire is in the foreground as the sergeant ensures the new tire's bead pops into place on the rim. Like every base, Luke Air Force Base has a large number of vehicles, which ensures the tire shop remains busy.

On August 27, 1973, Lt. Col. Thomas A. Rush (above), chief of the Instructional Systems Development Trainer in the 58th Training Squadron at Luke Air Force Base, shows a student how to operate the Instructional Systems Development Trainer F-4 Cockpit Procedures Trainer. Colonel Rush developed the trainer to help students learn to fly the F-4C. The system projects thousands of sound-on-slides from a projector onto a small screen that the student can see through the windscreen of the trainer. Behind the scenes, Maj. Roger Henry (below) checks one of those thousands of slides to ensure its accuracy. The trainer was more advanced than a simple mockup, but did not take up valuable simulator time.

On November 17, 1972, airmen occupied three new barracks, later called dormitories, at Luke Air Force Base. In the late 1960s and early 1970s, housing on the base was still a concern, with many airmen living in the old 1941 wooden barracks. The new barracks meant the old temporary World War II buildings could be torn down. (Photograph by Paul K. Smith.)

In 1972, a government civilian painter in the 58th Transportation Squadron paints a vehicle at Luke Air Force Base. The 58th Transportation Squadron painted vehicles based upon major sun damage and after doing bodywork. Certain large specialty vehicles, like cranes, spent decades in service. Painting vehicles protected them from corrosion, especially as they aged.

On August 21, 1973, Larry and Dorothy Schneider meet with Sgt. Robert Marusiak and Master Sgt. Albert Richmond for the second time in front of a Sikorsky H-34 Choctaw helicopter at Luke Air Force Base. Marusiak and Richmond were members of the Air Force Reserve's 302nd Aerospace Rescue and Recovery Squadron. On May 1, 1973, the four met for the first time during a helicopter mission when the airmen rescued the couple.

On May 18, 1973, F-4C, tail number 63-7510, approaches the runway while the runway supervisory officer watches from the runway supervisory unit at Luke Air Force Base. Aircrew serve as runway supervisory officers, later called the supervisor of flying, on a rotating basis. One of their duties is to ensure that pilots have their landing gear down and locked as they approach the airfield for touch-and-goes or landings.

On February 28, 1972, a staff sergeant in the welding shop welds an item at Luke Air Force Base. Depending upon the application, welders join two items together or repair cracks in items. As part of the 58th Field Maintenance Squadron Fabrication Flight, welding shop technicians work closely with those in the machine shop and sheet metal shops to create needed equipment and repair worn and damaged items.

In 1973, an airman in the consolidated base personnel office, later renamed the military personnel flight, searches for a personnel record. Every time a personnel action takes place, a clerk has to pull that person's record and attach the new paperwork. Hardcopy records remained the Air Force standard until the late 1980s and early 1990s, when computerized records began to replace them.

On December 5, 1974, a crew chief signals an F-5 pilot from the 425th Tactical Fighter Training Squadron to taxi out of the parking spot during the Turkey Shoot at Luke Air Force Base. Depending upon the capabilities of the aircraft's environmental system at taxi speeds and the weather, aircrews would often raise their canopies. With the canopy up, they got fresh air, but had to live with the jet noise.

In the fall of 1974, a flight of four F-4C aircraft takes off in formation to the southwest with the White Tank Mountains in the background. Taking off and flying in formation are important skills for every fighter pilot. Often, the final check ride is a four-ship mission. The two-ship is the basic combat formation. A four-ship formation is the basis for many advanced fighter tactics.

During the summer of 1974, Airman First Class Chris McMillin and Mr. Joaquin Ruiz of the 58th Field Maintenance Squadron at Luke Air Force Base work on an F-4 transfer gearbox. They are installing an afterburner fuel pump onto the transfer case; the gearbox provides the power to run the pump. Without a properly working fuel pump, the F-4's afterburner would not function correctly, possibly endangering the aircrew.

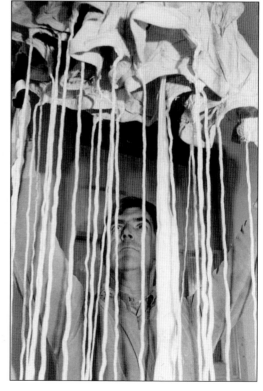

On February 4, 1975, a rigger in the egress shop at Luke Air Force Base checks a drogue chute to see if it is dry. Rarely used, aircrew parachutes remain pristine and require periodic inspection and repack. Drogue chutes are different. Drogue chutes stop aircraft like the F-4C upon landing. After use, drogue chutes are dirty and often worn. Prior to repack, riggers wash, dry, and inspect them for wear.

Luke Air Force Base's pre-1974 commissary (above), much like the World War II commissary, was in a converted warehouse. Prior to the start of the all-volunteer force in 1973, airmen's pay was a fraction of what it would later be. Therefore, the government subsidized commissary prices so products cost a fraction of commercial store prices. The arrival of the F-15 in 1974 brought a new commissary, built on the east side of Litchfield Road south of Thunderbird Road. The new commissary (below) was much larger. After airmen's pay rose, commissary prices did too. Those prices are now roughly equivalent with the big box stores. Just south of the new commissary is the new Base Exchange, which also opened in 1974. A large parking lot serves both the commissary and the Base Exchange.

Above, one of the most historic events in the history of Luke Air Force Base occurred on November 14, 1974. For the first time, a sitting president of the United States visited the base. Pres. Gerald R. Ford Jr. wanted to be at the arrival of the first McDonnell Douglas F-15A/B Eagle into the operational inventory. After President Ford's speech, he greeted the pilot (below). Gov. Jack Williams of Arizona is second from left. Brig. Gen. Fred A. Haeffner, 58th Tactical Fighter Training Wing commander, is directly behind Ford. At far right is Col. Francis Bloomcamp of the 4486th Test Squadron at Edwards Air Force Base, California, who flew in the rear cockpit. Between the two pilots is Gen. David C. Jones, Air Force chief of staff. Behind General Jones is Gen. Robert J. Dixon, commander of Tactical Air Command. (Above, photograph by Sgt. Brad McHargue; below, photograph by Technical Sgt. Ed Goodhue.)

Prior to President Ford's speech, Lt. Col. Ernest T. "Ted" Laudis taxied the F-15B aircraft, tail number 73-0108, also known as TAC-1, around Air Force One and parked at Luke Air Force Base. Laudis was the commander of the 555th Tactical Fighter Training Squadron. Later, Ford and Colonel Laudis walked around the aircraft. Above, Laudis stands under the left wing, probably telling the president about how the ailerons and high-lift flaps give the Eagle its maneuverability. Below, standing on the air stairs next to the aircraft, Laudis briefs the president on the cockpit layout and the Aces II ejection seat. (Both photographs by Technical Sgt. Ed Goodhue.)

In 1974, the new hospital at Luke Air Force Base opened east of Litchfield Road and north of Thunderbird Road. On December 5, 1974, Col. Leonard W. Johnson Jr., commander of the US Air Force Hospital Luke, stands in front of the new building, which faces Litchfield Road. The new building replaced numerous World War II buildings on the south end of the base. The old hospital location later became athletic fields.

During the winter of 1974, cars line up for gas at the Base Exchange's gas station, located north of the main gate. In October 1973, the Organization of the Petroleum Exporting Countries announced that its members were cutting oil production and placing an embargo on the United States. The embargo had an immediate effect on drivers across the country, leading to a four-fold price increase, gas rationing, and long lines.

Six

TACTICAL TRAINING LUKE AND 832ND AIR DIVISION
1977–1991

In the mid-1980s, looking east from the flight line, the 832nd Air Division leadership stands in front of its personnel at Luke Air Force Base. In the center is the F-15A/B/D flagship. To the sides are the two F-16 flagships. In flight above is a UH-1 Iroquois, better known as the Huey. For decades, the base had more fighter aircraft than any other base, earning the moniker "Fighter Country."

In the spring of 1980, three civil engineer specialists from Luke Air Force Base, two master sergeants and a technical sergeant, provide security during their Prime BEEF (Base Engineer Emergency Force) team's exercise at Luke Auxiliary Field 1, north of the White Tank Mountains in Arizona. Prime BEEF teams are rapidly deployable 25-man civil engineer teams that train and respond to contingencies worldwide. As part of that mission, they provide their own security.

In the summer of 1980, Airman Pamela Kassnel demonstrates her ability to handle a firehose during training at Luke Air Force Base. As more and more women entered the traditionally male occupations, the airmen's attitudes changed to "if she can do the job, including its physical demands, she is one of us."

On December 12, 1980, an instructor walks a class of weapons system officers through a mockup of the back seat of an F-4C at Luke Air Force Base. While the back seat had a stick and throttle, it also had a radar display (at top). The weapons system officers worked the radar and avionics. If the pilot became incapacitated, the back seater could take control of the aircraft.

In late 1979, aircrews process through the mobility line during an exercise at Luke Air Force Base. The first part of mobility is processing, which ensures all of the individual's training and travel documents are current. Next, airmen check all of an individual's clothing and equipment to make sure they are ready to deploy. Third is the packing of the unit's parts and equipment required for the deployment.

In 1980, airmen of the 58th Equipment Maintenance Squadron load a dart aerial gunnery target on an F-4C. Darts replaced the old rectangular cloth tow targets. Once in the target area, the tow plane would let the cable out until the dart was 1,500 feet or more behind the aircraft. Its shiny surfaces reflected radar beams, so it could be used for radar gunsights. Later, avionics would replace the darts for air-to-air gunnery.

In the summer of 1980, an explosive ordnance disposal team from Luke Air Force Base works to clear the Luke Air Force Range. Most of the ordnance these airmen are collecting are inert 500-pound MK-82 bombs being hauled off for disposal. If they find live ordnance, these airmen will dispose of it onsite or disarm it and move it to a disposal site.

In mid-February 1980, floodwaters caused major issues in the Salt River Valley. The Indian School Road bridge over the Agua Fria River near Luke Air Force Base was one of the victims. Indian School Road was one of the major arteries connecting the base to Phoenix. Floodwaters also took down nine of ten bridges across the Salt River. (Photograph by Staff Sgt. Bill Rigsby.)

On June 6, 1980, aircrews of the 58th Tactical Training Wing run to their alert F-4C aircraft during an air defense exercise at Luke Air Force Base. Alert has special rules for both aircrews and aircraft. As aircrews come on alert, they preflight the alert aircraft and set up the cockpits with their gear. Afterwards, with the aircraft quarantined, aircrews remain in the alert area or in the squadron.

In August 1981, Airman First Class Charles Woodring (left) and Staff Sgt. Steve Moore of the 58th Civil Engineering Squadron work on a broken water main at Luke Air Force Base. By that time, all of the temporary World War II underground infrastructure was 40 years old; parts of those systems were wearing out and needed replacement.

In October 1980, a civilian airman updates the sortie production sign at the front gate at Luke Air Force Base. The sign reflects the Production (later, Combat) Oriented Maintenance Organization philosophy. Under the original concept, when a wing's operations and maintenance organizations meet their mutual monthly sortie production goal, they take the last fly day of the month off, so they can accomplish non-flying tasks.

On November 4, 1982, the last of a huge fleet of F-4Cs leaves Luke Air Force Base as tail number 63-7510 lifts off for a new assignment at an Air National Guard unit. For 11 years, the 58th Tactical Fighter Training Wing (later the 58th Tactical Training Wing) provided combat aircrew training in the F-4 Phantom II (affectionately called "Old Double Ugly" by many), totaling 3,147 aircrew graduates.

A worker from the 58th Tactical Training Wing Maintenance Section at Luke Air Force Base prepares an F-4E flight simulator for shipment to its new home at Taegu Air Base, Korea. When the wing ended its role as an F-4 flying training unit, the simulator was an excess item. It turned out that across the world, a base on the Korean peninsula had a requirement for the simulator. (Photograph by Gustave Vinas.)

In the spring of 1981, a female crew chief checks on a line replaceable unit, or black box, on an F-15 in the 405th Tactical Training Wing at Luke Air Force Base. In the Air Force, flight line aircraft maintenance is one of the male-heavy career fields. Culturally, most females are drawn to other career fields.

In the spring of 1981, a 405th Component Repair Squadron F-15 avionics apprentice checks his technical data at Luke Air Force Base. After basic training, airmen go to a technical school to learn the basics of their career fields. At their first base, they go through a career-specific development course to become journeymen. For avionics specialists, their career development course takes about 18 months to complete.

On December 6, 1982, an F-16 Fighting Falcon, tail number 78-0081, arrives at Luke Air Force Base. It was the first F-16 permanently assigned to the 58th Tactical Training Wing; 56 Fighting Falcons were destined for the wing in its new role of providing aircrew training in the F-16, which began on January 1, 1983.

In the winter of 1983, a technical sergeant leads a team of US Air Force Hospital Luke airmen as they wheel a patient with a simulated injury into the emergency room during an exercise at Luke Air Force Base. Although the hospital changed organizational hands a number of times, it remained a full-service hospital until September 28, 2005, when it closed its ambulatory procedures unit and operating rooms.

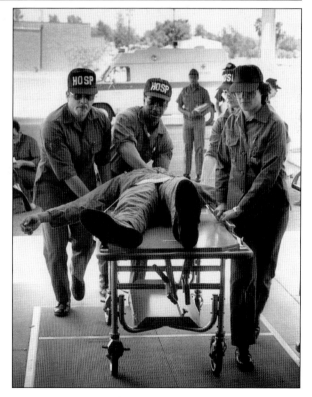

Above, on March 16, 1983, after Class 82-DBL's final flight, made up of eight F-104G Starfighters, there was a ceremony upon landing at Luke Air Force Base. With that class's landing, the US Air Force–German air force training program came to an end. Making the final inspection and giving the final salute are, from left to right, Lt. Gen. Friedrich Obleser, German air force chief of staff; Gen. Wilber L. Creech, Tactical Air Command commander; Lt. Col. Heinrich Thuringer, German air force 2nd Training Squadron commander; and Lt. Col. Robert A. Patterson, 69th Tactical Fighter Training Squadron commander. Below, on June 1, 1983, the last F-104G Starfighter leaves Luke Air Force Base bound for Taiwan after the Taiwanese government purchased the aircraft.

On November 15, 1984, the 58th Tactical Fighter Training Wing held a ceremony at Luke Air Force Base celebrating the arrival of the first F-16C (single-seater, left) and F-16D (two-seater, right) models into the Air Force's operational inventory. On October 1, 1984, the 312nd Tactical Fighter Training Squadron activated as the first F-16C/D squadron. Its mission was to train students to fly the aircraft. (Photograph by Gustave Vinas.)

In the fall of 1983, an F-16 student in the 311th Tactical Fighter Training Squadron at Luke Air Force Base reviews a mission film. A camera mounted on his F-16 took the film. The student notes the things he did right and wrong. By analyzing those things, he will figure out how to improve his performance. (Photograph by Gustave Vinas.)

In 1985, this sergeant in the 2037th Information Services Squadron Data Automation Branch was a computer operator at Luke Air Force Base. She is preparing to put a magnetic tape reel into the Phase IV system, which serviced all the data-processing requirements for units on base, as well as the supply requirements of Williams Air Force Base and elements of the Arizona Air National Guard. (Photograph by Gustave Vinas.)

On August 16, 1985, members of the 405th Tactical Training Wing assembled on the flight line at Luke Air Force Base to form a huge 200,000 to mark the 200,000th flying hour at the base. Col. Thomas C. Skanchy, commander of the 405th Tactical Training Wing, flew the landmark hour. The F-15s reached the milestone in less than 11 years.

On September 27, 1985, the F-16
Demonstration Team's primary
members pose for a group photograph
on top of one of the team's Fighting
Falcons at Luke Air Force Base.
The team's pilot, Capt. Ronald
Oholendt, stands on the left. Capt.
Richard Thomas, the team's narrator,
stands on the right. Both fly with
the 311th Tactical Fighter Training
Squadron. During the fiscal year, the
team performed at 20 air shows.

During the second week of December
1985, two airmen tighten the cargo
straps on a 463L pallet, which their
unit built as part of a mobility
inspection at Luke Air Force
Base. The Tactical Air Command
Management Effectiveness Inspection
Team conducted the inspection.
The Air Force expects units with
mobility commitments to be ready
to deploy anywhere in the world
within hours of notification.

On January 9, 1987, an F-16, tail number 79-0303, from Luke Air Force Base hit a bird, cracking the outer layer of the canopy and injuring the pilot. Maj. Homer Smith of the 310th Tactical Fighter Training Squadron successfully landed his damaged aircraft. Bird strikes are always dangerous, especially for single-engine aircraft like the F-16. If a bird hits an F-16's engine, the base may lose an aircraft.

On July 8, 1986, Capt. George A. Sousa of the 312th Tactical Fighter Training Squadron flies the new F-16C simulator on a test mission. Both Col. Joseph C. Rively (far left) and Col. Brian E. Wages, from the 58th Tactical Training Wing, watch, as does Ross A. Miles (far right), the Singer-Link district sales manager. The system projects computer models of the actual surrounding countryside onto screens, giving a feeling that is closer to actual flight.

In the spring of 1986, an 832nd Security Police Squadron airman mans the main gate at Luke Air Force Base. During the 1980s, many bases replaced their old guard shacks with a new design known for its 360-degree view that gave gate guards the ability to see traffic leaving the base as well as coming on-base. This location is currently underneath the Maj. Troy Gilbert Bridge. (Photograph by Gustave Vinas.)

In 1987, four F-16C/D aircraft sit on the 944th Tactical Fighter Group's aircraft parking ramp, which is well west of the west ramp at Luke Air Force Base. Some of the group's facilities are still under construction. On July 1, 1987, the Air Force Reserve reactivated the redesignated 944th Tactical Fighter Group at Luke Air Force Base to fly 15 F-16C/Ds.

On October 5, 1987, the 405th Tactical Training Wing holds a ceremony on the flight line near the fire department to commemorate the stand-down of its helicopter operations section at Luke Air Force Base. The section had three UH-1 Iroquois, better known as the Huey, and boasted 16 accident-free years flying helicopters. The stand-down resulted from budgetary constraints.

On July 18, 1988, the 405th Tactical Training Wing holds a ceremony in Hangar 431 at Luke Air Force Base to officially mark the start of F-15E Strike Eagle training in the 461st Tactical Fighter Training Squadron. On March 3, 1988, the squadron ceased its F-15A/B/D operations in order to prepare for Strike Eagle operations. On April 12, 1988, the first F-15E, tail number 86-0186, arrived at the base. (Photograph by Gustave Vinas.)

In late 1989, an airman of the 832nd Supply Squadron holds the dead-man's switch of his R-11 refueler truck while he refuels an F-15E Strike Eagle in the 461st Aircraft Maintenance Unit at Luke Air Force Base. The Oshkosh Truck Corporation made the R-11. In 1989, the Air Force began replacing its old R-9 refueler trucks with the new R-11, which became its primary mobile refueling vehicle.

In October 1989, the 832nd Combat Support Group Headquarters took possession of the Blockhouse, Building 1150, at Luke Air Force Base. The previous North American Air Defense Command facility required a complete renovation because its new functions were so different from its previous functions. The building holds several headquarter staff agencies and several subordinate units of the 832nd Combat Support Group. (Photograph by Gustave Vinas.)

On October 5, 1989, Soviet defense minister Gen. Dmitry T. Yazov visited Luke Air Force Base. His host was Lt. Gen. Peter T. Kempf, 12th Air Force commander. General Kempf was a previous 58th Tactical Training Wing commander at Luke Air Force Base. The historic visit was due to the warming relations between the United States and the Soviet Union.

On August 29, 1989, Lt. Col. Michael Rickman of the 425th Tactical Fighter Training Squadron flew tail number 73-0881 (pictured) on the last F-5E mission for the squadron. It was a continuing training sortie. Eighty-five percent of the F-5's parts are the same as the T-38; it flew from Williams Air Force Base but organizationally belonged to Luke Air Force Base due to their similar missions. (Photograph by Gustave Vinas.)

In late 1989, Lt. Col. John E. Chambers, commander of the 310th Tactical Fighter Training Squadron, and Senior Master Sgt. Robert Carter, of the 310th Aircraft Maintenance Unit, inspect a Low Altitude Navigation and Targeting Infrared for Night (LANTIRN) pod on an F-16C Block 42 aircraft. On June 9, 1989, the squadron flew the first LANTIRN sortie at Luke Air Force Base. The F-15E Strike Eagle units followed later in the year.

During Operation Desert Shield/Storm, 405th Tactical Training Wing airmen flew 258 combat missions. From left to right, Capt. William M. Mullins flew 40 F-15E combat missions, Maj. William Chamblee flew 20, and Lt. Col. Keith Trumbull flew 38. Of the F-16 LANTIRN and F-15E aircrews in Operation Desert Shield/Storm, 100 percent of them trained at Luke Air Force Base, as did a large number of the F-15A/B/C/D pilots and F-16 aircrew.

The F-15E Strike Eagle flagship of the 405th Tactical Training Wing at Luke Air Force Base leads a formation of its squadrons' flagships over the desert. The darker grey F-15E aircraft are the flagships of the 461st and 550th Tactical Fighter Training Squadrons. The lighter grey aircraft are the air superiority F-15A Eagle flagships of the 555th and 426th Tactical Fighter Training Squadrons.

In late 1987, the flagship of the 58th Tactical Training Wing leads its squadrons' flagships in formation flying to the northwest. Below are the parallel runways of Luke Air Force Base. From nearest to farthest are the flagships from the 311th Tactical Fighter Training Squadron, 310th Tactical Fighter Training Squadron, 58th Tactical Training Wing, 312th Tactical Fighter Training Squadron, and 314th Tactical Fighter Training Squadron.

130

Seven

58TH FIGHTER WING
1991–1994

On December 20, 1991, the last McDonnell Douglas F-15A Eagle left Luke Air Force Base. With the takeoff of the light gray F-15, tail number 76-0028, the F-15A/B/C/D program ended at the base. During its time here, four squadrons flew the light grey F-15: the 426th, 461st, 550th, and 555th Tactical Fighter Training Squadrons. Since 1974, the program produced 3,303 American and allied graduates.

A staff sergeant holds the guidance and control unit of a captive short-range AIM-9 Sidewinder training missile at Luke Air Force Base. The other airman prepares to torque it into place. Both work in the 58th Maintenance Squadron Munitions Flight. Once the AIM-9 became a standard short-range air-to-air weapon, most pilot training missions carried one. By then, avionics replaced towed targets for air-to-air gunnery practice.

A captain in the Medical Corps listens to a military patient's vital signs at Luke Air Force Base. Based upon their battle dress uniforms, this photograph was taken during the early 1990s, when the Luke Air Force Base Hospital fell under the 58th Medical Group. During that time, the hospital offered both in-patient and out-patient care along with an emergency room.

On October 1, 1991, from left to right, Lt. Gen. Thomas A. Baker, 12th Air Force commander, helps Brig. Gen. Ralph T. Browning furl the colors of the 832nd Air Division at Luke Air Force Base. The 832nd Air Division and 405th Tactical Training Wing inactivated as part of a major reorganization. During its 12 years at the base, the wing graduated over 2,626 F-15, F-15E Strike Eagle, and F-5 students.

On October 1, 1991, Tactical Air Command reorganized Luke Air Force Base. As Col. William T. Hobbins (left), the new vice commander, looks on, Brig. Gen. Ralph T. Browning, the new 58th Fighter Wing commander, receives the flag of the newly redesignated wing from Lt. Gen. Thomas A. Baker, 12th Air Force commander. Part of the reorganization inactivated the aircraft generation squadrons and moved flight line maintenance into the fighter squadrons.

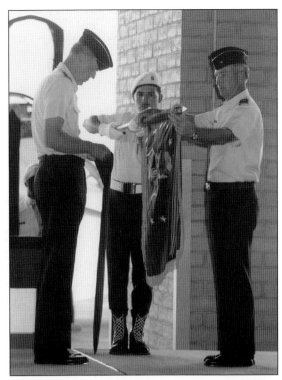

Brig. Gen. Ralph T. Browning was a prisoner of war in North Vietnam between July 8, 1966, and February 12, 1973. He was the only known person to hold four commands at Luke Air Force Base. He commanded the 555th Tactical Fighter Training Squadron, the 58th Tactical Training Wing, the 832nd Air Division, and on October 1, 1991, the 58th Fighter Wing, when the Air Force eliminated air divisions.

In the early 1990s, two airmen work on an engine module in the jet engine intermediate maintenance shop at Luke Air Force Base. Both F-15s and F-16s flew variations of the Pratt & Whitney F100 engine. Unlike early engines, the F100 was modular. The Air Force allowed the intermediate shops to separate and reconnect the modules as well as add engine accessories and fuel and electrical harnesses.

On October 20, 1992, intense storms hit the local area. On the north side of Luke Air Force Base, the Dysart Drainage Canal overflowed, collapsing the fence and flooding both the operations and housing sides of base. Above, looking west from over the housing area, flooding extends across the airfield. On the north end of the north aircraft parking ramp, small rocks and dirt filled F-15E brake stacks. At the junctions of the aircraft parking ramps, the water was deeper, with rocks in F-16 afterburner sections. The 314th Aircraft Maintenance Unit had 14 inches of water inside the building. The damage caused the base to cancel flying for a couple of days. Below, people carry their children across a flooded Thunderbird Street from the hospital parking lot toward the commissary parking lot. Housing area damage totaled $3 million.

The sheet metal shop at Luke Air Force Base is a busy place. On the left, a government civilian uses a hand grinder on a project. At far right, an airman drills holes in an engine nacelle. Standing to the left of him, another airman works on F-16 aircraft ladders. Above the work benches, the white jars reduce the moisture in the compressed air, helping the tools to last longer.

A staff sergeant in the jet engine intermediate maintenance shop's supply room at Luke Air Force Base picks up an incoming box of parts in the early 1990s. In the 1980s, the Air Force leadership decided to spread the supply function into the maintenance areas instead of at a centralized location on base. The Air Force called those forward supply points the Combat Oriented Supply Organization.

On March 12, 1993, at the ceremony marking assumption of command of the 63rd Fighter Squadron at Luke Air Force Base, Brig. Gen. Patrick K. Gamble (left), 58th Fighter Wing commander, hands the guidon to the new commander, Lt. Col. William H. Christian Jr. On February 25, 1993, the squadron was the first 56th Fighter Wing unit to move from MacDill Air Force Base, Florida, to Luke Air Force Base.

On March 20, 1993, the first F-16A/B aircraft leased by the Singapore air force for the Peace Carvin II program arrived at Luke Air Force Base. Lt. Col. Wayne E. Hughes, 425th Fighter Squadron commander, is exiting the aircraft. His back seater is Lt. Col. Richard Lim, the Singapore air force senior representative. On December 30, 1992, the squadron reactivated to conduct continuation training for Singapore's F-16 pilots.

The sign at the main gate of Luke Air Force Base welcomes all visitors to the base. Tan sump blocks surround the sign and create its base. Many of the buildings constructed in the 1970s and 1980s used tan sump block for their exterior walls. Even the base's exterior fence along the west side of Litchfield Road is tan sump block.

On July 1, 1993, the Air Force reassigned Luke Air Force Base from Air Combat Command to the newly redesignated Air Education and Training Command. At the ceremony, from left to right, 2nd Lt. Shae Armstrong looks on as Lt. Col. Jack L. Baily Jr., the narrator, helps Col. David L. Sonnenberg, the 58th Fighter Wing vice commander, unveil the Air Education and Training Command emblem.

The crew chief helps 1st Lt. Jeannie M. Flynn buckle in a McDonnell Douglas F-15E Strike Eagle. Lieutenant Flynn was the first female fighter pilot in US Air Force history. On February 10, 1994, she completed her basic course with the 555th Fighter Squadron. Later, she married, and in 2016, the Air Force promoted Colonel Leavitt to brigadier general.

At Luke Air Force Base, the 461st Fighter Squadron, commanded by Lt. Col. John M. Carter Jr., stands in front of the wing and squadron flagships, tail numbers 87-0185 and 86-0187 respectively. Behind the flagships is the squadron's aircraft maintenance building, Building 460. To the east is the squadron's operations building, Building 461. Colonel Carter commanded the squadron from January 15, 1993, until it inactivated on August 5, 1994.

On April 1, 1994, vice wing commander Col. James Brechwald and wing Chief Master Sgt. Clarence Miller furl the 58th Fighter Wing's flag at Luke Air Force Base, signaling its departure after 24 years. Military flags are symbolic of the organizations they represent and are furled when the units close or depart and unfurled when they activate or arrive. Since October 15, 1969, the 58th called Luke Air Force Base home.

On April 1, 1994, wing Chief Master Sgt. Billy Gerald holds and vice wing commander Col. James Brechwald unfurls the 56th Fighter Wing's flag, signaling its arrival at Luke Air Force Base. The 56th Fighter Wing is one of the most highly decorated units in aviation history. Its arrival signified the beginning of the longest time any wing spent at the base.

Eight

56TH FIGHTER WING
1994–2019

In 2005, the 56th Fighter Wing at Luke Air Force Base was the world's largest fighter unit, with eight fighter squadrons assigned and boasting an aerial fleet made up of 189 F-16 Fighting Falcons in Fighter County. Those squadrons were the 21st, 61st, 62nd, 63rd, 308th, 309th, 310th, and 425th Fighter Squadrons. Between 1996 and 2015, all eight squadrons flew at Luke Air Force Base.

Moving to Luke Air Force Base, the 56th Fighter Wing Headquarters took up residence in Building S-11, where it would remain until June 13, 2001. Its subordinate units reactivated at Luke Air Force Base on April 1, 1994, replacing the 58 numbered units. The 311th and 314th Fighter Squadrons inactivated in order to activate 61st and 62nd Fighter Squadrons. Additionally, four new squadrons activated in the 56th Medical Group.

Looking northeast from the control tower in the mid- to late 1990s, the west aircraft parking ramp at Luke Air Force Base is full of F-16s. The 63rd Fighter Squadron's F-16s are parked on the south aircraft parking ramp. Out of sight farther south of that squadron was the 425th Fighter Squadron. During the early 1990s, both F-15E squadrons flew from the north aircraft parking ramp.

On September 21, 1994, Capt. Sharon Preszler graduated from the 61st Fighter Squadron at Luke Air Force Base, becoming the first female F-16 pilot in the US Air Force. As a fighter pilot, she flew over Iraq in Operation Northern Watch. In 2006, Lieutenant Colonel Preszler retired from the Air Force.

On March 21, 1995, the last F-15E Strike Eagle, tail number 87-0186, departs Luke Air Force to the northeast, with the Estrella Mountains in the background, ending the Strike Eagle's seven-year stay. During that time, the Strike Eagle graduated 897 aircrew. The aircraft is already painted with its new base's markings. That departure also signaled the end of the 21-year tenure of F-15s at the base.

On September 11, 1996, Pres. William J. "Bill" Clinton talks to members of the 56th Security Forces Squadron and other airmen at Luke Air Force Base. President Clinton was the second sitting president to visit the base, now the largest F-16 base in the world.

On August 27, 1997, the US Fish and Wildlife Service issued an opinion that air operations on the Barry M. Goldwater Range likely did not jeopardize the continued existence of Sonoran pronghorn antelope. Previously, environmentalist groups charged that air-to-ground missions from bases like Luke Air Force Base jeopardized the endangered species, which prompted the Fish and Wildlife Service's opinion.

On August 8, 1996, Col. Gilmary M. Hostage III, 56th Operations Group commander, hands the reactivating 21st Fighter Squadron's guidon to its new commander, Lt. Col. James R. "Rusty" Mitchell, at Luke Air Force Base. The 21st Fighter Squadron's mission is to train Taiwan air force pilots to fly the F-16 under the United States' Foreign Military Sales program. Later, that mission changed to continuation training for Taiwan air force pilots.

On June 2, 1998, the first two Block 52 F-16s, aircraft tail numbers 94-0276 (the two-seat D model pictured here) and 94-0266 (a single-seat C model), arrived at Luke Air Force Base. Both were assigned to the 425th Fighter Squadron as an upgrade to the Peace Carvin II program for the Republic of Singapore, which was flying Block 42 F-16s.

On September 25, 1999, the 56th Fighter Wing hosted a civilian fly-in at Luke Air Force Base to stress flight safety to civilian pilots. During the fly-in, airmen briefed about 350 attendees on the base's operations, time and distance separation requirements, and the unit's mid-air collision avoidance program. Since 1980, Luke Air Force Base has periodically hosted civilian fly-in days.

An F-16 F100 engine runs in full afterburner on the Hush House test cell. In the late 1990s, the F-16 community ran into problems with the turbofans of the F100 engines. With the F-16 being a single-engine aircraft, any engine issue can be a major problem. Once the engineers determined the proper repair, the test cell was kept busy testing the modified engines.

On March 8, 2000, 1st Lt. Joshua Padgett inspects an F-16 prior to flight. Lieutenant Padgett completed the basic course with the 62nd Fighter Squadron and became Luke Air Force Base host units' 50,000th graduate. The base host units started their formal syllabus fighter training courses in June 1941.

On March 3, 2000, the 301st Fighter Squadron held its activation ceremony as part of the 944th Fighter Wing at Luke Air Force Base. Officially activated on January 1, 2000, the squadron implemented the Associate F-16 Instructor Pilot Program. Under the program, while the unit was assigned to the 944th Fighter Wing, the squadron operationally fell under the control of the 56th Operations Group.

In the early 2000s, a man waits for a new identification card at the pass and identification office at Luke Air Force Base. The office is in the Blockhouse, Building 1150. The sergeant enters his information into the computer system. After she prints out the paper copies of his identification cards, she will run them through the card laminator to her left.

On June 21, 2001, the new $3.8-million control tower went into operation at Luke Air Force Base (right). On the west end of the west aircraft parking ramp, the new control tower is east of the old control tower (left), built in 1972. The air traffic controllers in the control tower direct all aircraft traffic on and immediately around Luke Air Force Base.

On September 19, 2001, to help at the World Trade Center, the 452nd Air Mobility Wing loads 60 Phoenix-area firefighters into C-141s at Luke Air Force Base. Due to the terrorist attacks, the base went to its highest level of force protection, launched 27 combat air patrol missions over the Phoenix area, and later deployed hundreds of people in support of the war on terrorism.

Looking to the southeast in the early 2000s, four F-16 flagships fly over Luke Air Force Base. From left to right are the 56th Operations Group and the 308th, 309th, and 310th Fighter Squadrons' flagships. Being a fly day, many of the parking spots below are empty. North of the baseball fields stands the gymnasium. The buildings directly north of the gymnasium and east of the pool are the temporary lodging facility.

On March 28, 2001, Arizona governor Jane Dee Hull signs Arizona Revised Statutes Title 28, Transportation Section 28-8481, which protects military airfields in Arizona, like Luke Air Force Base. The law was one of the first by a state to protect military airfields. It called for compatible use of the land around the airfields. Arizona later followed up with other legislation increasing those protections.

On July 11, 2003, a rebuilt Ocotillo Manor base housing complex south of Glendale Avenue opened for occupancy with 95 new units at Luke Air Force Base. In 2001, residents in all 150 units vacated that housing area in preparation for demolition and construction of the new complex. On February 6, 2007, all base housing transferred to a civilian firm under the Air Force's privatization program.

In 2004, a civilian contract security force guard checks the identification of an individual entering Luke Air Force Base. Luke Air Force Base uses a civilian contract security force to help the 56th Security Force Squadron guard the base. Reduced manning over the years combined with periodic deployments of large portions of the squadron led to a shortfall in security forces. The civilian contractor fills the gap.

On August 29, 2005, Pres. George W. Bush and his wife, Laura, visited Luke Air Force Base. While here, they visited with airmen on the base and people in El Mirage, Arizona. Bush was the third sitting president to visit the base.

Looking east-northeast from the control tower in 2005, the west aircraft parking ramp at Luke Air Force Base is full of sunshades cooling the F-16s. The sunshades are metal frames covered with fabric. While the shade moves during the day based on the location of the sun, aircraft under the sunshades stay significantly cooler than those parked in the full sun.

On November 26, 2012, an airman installs a panel on the back of an F-16 under the sunshades at Luke Air Force Base. The panels structurally required for flight have lots of screws. A panel may take more than one size screw. The airman is using a speed handle fitted with an apex for the specific screw he is tightening. (Photograph by Staff Sgt. Jason Colbert.)

On October 23, 2012, 1st Lt. Cayce Wilkins checks the BDU-33 practice bombs on a triple ejector rack on his F-16 prior to flight at Luke Air Force Base. The triple ejector rack allows aircraft to carry more ordnance than just a bomb on each pylon. Given all that is invested to get a student to the range, being able to drop more bombs while there increases that student's training. (Photograph by Staff Sgt. Jason Colbert.)

On April 18, 2012, a sergeant air traffic controller checks the overhead screen for information in the control tower at Luke Air Force Base. This photograph was taken looking to the northeast. Outside, it is a bright day, so the air traffic controllers have pulled down the tinted window shades. No aircraft are visible on the runways or the taxiways.

On August 23, 2012, 56th Civil Engineer Squadron fire emergency services members assess the scene before removing the simulated victims during an exercise on Luke Air Force Base. This exercise involves an upside-down car in a flood control ditch during severe weather. Exercise planners work to come up with realistic exercise events for the various on- and off-base agencies to respond to. (Photograph by Senior Airman Sandra Welch.)

On January 11, 2012, Airman Shawn Delory of the 56th Logistics Readiness Squadron pulls a fuel sample from an R-11 refueler truck at Luke Air Force Base. Pulling fuel samples is common and typically is used to check for contamination in the fuel. To guarantee flight safety, all equipment related to any incident is quarantined and samples tested. That equipment is released once its samples come back clean. (Photograph by Staff Sgt. Jason Colbert.)

On January 3, 2013, Shaunn Feazel, a 56th Civil Engineer Squadron dispatcher, monitors screens in the emergency control center at Luke Air Force Base. The center is one of four certified public safety answering points in the greater Phoenix metropolitan area. It responds to on- and off-base emergencies, answers all 911 emergency calls, and acts as a command and control point for emergency responders. (Photograph by Staff Sgt. Jason Colbert.)

On March 13, 2013, 1st Lt. Matthew J. Wetherbee, a 309th Fighter Squadron student, flies the one-millionth F-16 Fighting Falcon flying hour by US squadrons at Luke Air Force Base. Given that flying 100,000 hours is a substantial achievement, flying a million hours is a major accomplishment. At Luke Air Force Base, it took the F-16s just over 30 years to reach that mark. (Photograph by A1C Devante Williams.)

On August 28, 2014, after airmen download an F-16 gun system, technicians organize 20-millimeter target practice ammunition in the 56th Equipment Maintenance Squadron Weapons Storage Area at Luke Air Force Base. While the target practice cartridge has no additional pyrotechnics in the projectile, it is still a live round. Therefore, accountability is important. Organizing the rounds into groups of 10 makes counting them easier. (Photograph by A1C James Hensley.)

On April 15, 2013, firefighters with the 56th Civil Engineer Squadron enter the "immediately dangerous to life and health zone" during a night fire training event at Luke Air Force Base. As they go, they begin to put out ground fires. The firefighters practice their skills on the fire training grounds at the base. (Photograph by Senior Airman Sandra Welch.)

On March 11, 2014, Col. Rodney Petithomme, 54th Fighter Group commander, speaks at the group's activation ceremony at Holloman Air Force Base, New Mexico. Stationed there, the group is assigned to the 56th Fighter Wing at Luke Air Force Base. Three squadrons were also activated: the 311th Fighter, 54th Operations Support, and 54th Aircraft Maintenance Squadrons. Later, the group added two more flying training squadrons before transferring to the 49th Wing. (Photograph by Senior Airman Daniel E. Liddicoet.)

On November 5, 2013, attending Dorothy Rowe's retirement ceremony at Luke Air Force Base are, from left to right, acting secretary of the Air Force Eric K. Fanning; retired Brig. Gen. Tom Browning, former Luke Air Force Base commander; Jerry Weiers, mayor of Glendale; and David Scholl, chairman of the board of Fighter Country Partnership. Rowe spent most of her 70-year career working for the base comptroller. (Photograph by A1C Pedro Mota.)

On March 10, 2014, the first Lockheed Martin F-35A Lightning II, tail number 11-5030, arrived at Luke Air Force Base. Col. Roderick L. Cregier, 412th Test Wing F-35 program director and test pilot, taxis the aircraft to its parking spot. The aircraft is assigned to 61st Aircraft Maintenance Unit, 56th Aircraft Maintenance Squadron. The Air Force projects putting up to six squadrons totaling 144 F-35A aircraft at the base. (Photograph by Staff Sgt. Darlene Seltmann.)

On March 15, 2014, crowds gather at Luke Air Force Base on the first day of a two-day open house. Over 300,000 people attended. In Brig. Gen. Michael D. Rothstein's opinion, the high attendance was due to two factors. First was the chance to see the base's first permanently assigned F-35A. Second, due to sequestration, this was the base's first open house in three years. (Photograph by Senior Airman Devante Williams.)

On June 16, 2015, F-16 Fighting Falcons from the 308th Fighter Squadron line up at the north end of the runway at Luke Air Force Base. The 12-aircraft launch took place to move the aircraft to their new home at Holloman Air Force Base, New Mexico. A month later, they would become part of the 314th Fighter Squadron of the 54th Fighter Group. Nine more F-16s left for Holloman the next day. (Photograph by Technical Sgt. Timothy S. Boyer.)

On March 4, 2016, Maj. William Andreotta, F-35 Heritage Flight Team pilot, salutes his team after a flight during the Heritage Flight Conference at Davis-Monthan Air Force Base in Tucson, Arizona. Luke Air Force Base's is the first F-35 team to participate in the Heritage Flight Program, which features modern fighter aircraft flying alongside World War II–, Korea-, and Vietnam-era aircraft displaying America's airpower history. (Photograph by Staff Sgt. Staci Miller.)

DISCOVER THOUSANDS OF LOCAL HISTORY BOOKS
FEATURING MILLIONS OF VINTAGE IMAGES

Arcadia Publishing, the leading local history publisher in the United States, is committed to making history accessible and meaningful through publishing books that celebrate and preserve the heritage of America's people and places.

Find more books like this at
www.arcadiapublishing.com

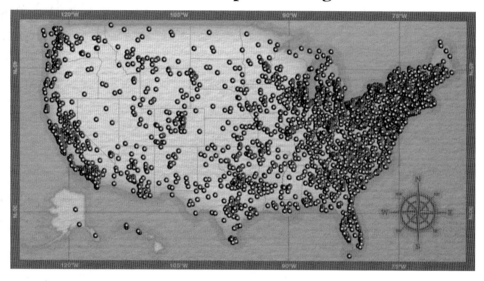

Search for your hometown history, your old stomping grounds, and even your favorite sports team.